The Horary Reference Book

The Horary Reference Book
Volume I

Anne Ungar
and
Lillian Huber

International Standard Book Number 0-917086-60-0

Cover Design by Laurie Ortiz

Printed in the United States of America

Published by ACS Publications, Inc.
P.O. Box 16430
San Diego, CA 92116-0430

First printing, July, 1984
Second printing, October, 1985

DEDICATION

To our husbands,
IRA UNGAR and CHARLES HUBER

without whose encouragement,
support, and patience
this book might never have been completed.

And to our children,

LILLIAN UNGAR   CHUCK HUBER
JULIE UNGAR   PATRICIA HUBER
and   and
DAVID UNGAR   JOE HUBER

who learned to be self-sufficient while
their mothers were becoming authors.

Also by ACS Publications, Inc.

All About Astrology Series
The American Atlas: US Latitudes and Longitudes, Time Changes
   and Time Zones (Shanks)
The American Book of Charts (Rodden)
The American Book of Nutrition & Medical Astrology (Nauman)
The American Book of Tables
The American Ephemeris Series 1901-2000
The American Ephemeris for the 20th Century [Midnight] 1900 to 2000
The American Ephemeris for the 20th Century [Noon] 1900 to 2000
The American Ephemeris for the 21st Century 2001 to 2100
The American Heliocentric Ephemeris 1901-2000
The American Sidereal Ephemeris 1976-2000
The Asteroid Ephemeris: Dudu, Dembowska, Pittsburgh, & Frigga
   (Stark & Pottenger)
Astrological Insights into Personality (Lundsted)
Astrological Predictions: A Revolutionary New Technique (Whitney)
Astrology: Old Theme, New Thoughts (March & McEvers)
Basic Astrology: A Guide for Teachers & Students (Negus)
Basic Astrology: A Workbook for Students (Negus)
The Body Says Yes (Kapel)
The Cosmic Clocks (M. Gauquelin)
Cosmic Combinations: A Book of Astrological Exercises (Negus)
Expanding Astrology's Universe (Dobyns)
The Fortunes of Astrology: A New Complete Treatment of the
   Arabic Parts (Granite)
The Gauquelin Book of American Charts (F. and M. Gauquelin)
The Gold Mine in Your Files (King)
Healing with the Horoscope: A Guide to Counseling (Pottenger)
Horoscopes of the Western Hemisphere (Penfield)
Instant Astrology (Orser & Brightfields)
The International Atlas: World Latitudes, Longitudes and
   Time Changes (Shanks)
Interpreting the Eclipses (Jansky)
The Koch Book of Tables
The Lively Circle (Koval)
The Mystery of Personal Identity (Mayer)
The Only Way to...Learn Astrology, Vol. I
   Basic Principles (March & McEvers)
The Only Way to...Learn Astrology, Vol. II
   Math & Interpretation Techniques (March & McEvers)
The Only Way to...Learn Astrology, Vol. III
   Horoscope Analysis (March & McEvers)
Planetary Planting (Riotte)
Planting by the Moon 1983/84 including Grower's Guide (Best &
   Kollerstrom)
The Psychic and the Detective (Druffel with Marcotte)
Psychology of the Planets (F. Gauquelin)
Secrets of the Palm (Hansen)
Small Ecstasies (Owens)
Stalking the Wild Orgasm (Kilham)
Tomorrow Knocks (Brunton)
12 Times 12 (McEvers)

TABLE OF CONTENTS

PREFACE

Horary astrology is one of the most ancient forms of astrology. This branch of astrology helps us to find the answer to a question in a chart cast for the moment the question is asked. Many of the rules of horary have been unnecessarily abstruse and hard to understand while some information useful for modern living was not available.

Our intention is to help bring the practice of horary astrology into the twenty-first century. There is nothing new in astrology, but we feel that there is a wealth of information waiting to be rediscovered. We have studied the subject in depth, and in the course of our investigation we sought logical reasons for the ancient horary rules and practices. Thus, we were able to clarify some of the horary rulerships and innovate new approaches to the derivative house system. Having gained a clearer grasp of the reasoning behind various methods used in horary, we can logically fit modern issues, principles and questions into this ancient framework.

The astrologer's success in reading the horary chart lies in choosing the appropriate house in which to place the question. It is through this choice that the significators (planetary rulers) of the question are chosen. Using the significator of an improper house will result in a false and erroneous reading. The astrologer, however, is often caught up in controversies regarding house rulerships and many of these controversies have not been resolved, even up to the present time.

We have checked many sources and have tried to incorporate into this volume a consensus of opinion, as well as share some ideas which have occurred to us. By ascertaining the underlying logic for many procedures in horary, we have been able to apply that same logic in some contested areas. While we do not feel qualified to arbitrate between respected astrological authorities, at least we hope to shed some light upon controversial issues.

Although the subject matter of this book is primarily horary astrology, this book will be helpful in any branch of astrology. The novice will find it invaluable as a general rulership book. Furthermore, the beginner will find the rules of horary astrology documented in a clear step-by-step manner which we hope will clarify the often obscure and archaic language of ancient horary books. The astrologer who wishes to become more proficient in the practice of horary astrology will have a ready reference to assist in locating the proper significators of the question. Additionally, new insights into the derivative house system and the application of the stepping system will help to eliminate confusion in the selection of the proper horary house.

Our primary goal was to compile a dictionary of horary house rulerships, thereby assuring the practicing astrologer of a greater degree of accuracy in locating proper significators. In this respect, we hope we have succeeded.

Horary astrology is less overwhelming than it appears. However, as one progresses in the study of this ancient art/science, there are other refinements to consider. We are planning another volume which will complement this one and will cover the finer nuances in more detail.

Horary astrology is a subject of ongoing research. We invite the reader to contact us, sharing ideas, opinions and charts which will either challenge or support our findings.

Anne Ungar and Lillian Huber

PART I

AN INTRODUCTION
TO HORARY ASTROLOGY

HORARY ASTROLOGY

The Chaldeans of Babylonia, whose civilization dates back to the eighteenth century BC, are credited with the origin of astrology. The Chaldeans believed that astrology was a religion and the planets were gods. The planetary gods, who resided in the heavens, ordered human life and their message could be read in the positions of the stars. The ancients viewed the visible astronomical bodies as gods who could affect or influence the fate of royalty and nations; therefore, the oldest form of astrology has a fated connotation.

Horary astrology is the oldest form of astrology. It deals with specific questions and specific answers to those questions. Horary astrology depicts the concrete circumstances of life. Consequently, the houses of the horary chart assume vital importance.

Horary astrology is founded upon the inherent dualism which exists in life. The play of opposites is apparent when one considers night and day, man and woman, and positive and negative. The existence of a problem implies that the solution to that problem exists. Furthermore, the existence of a question implies that the answer to that question exists. This answer can be read in the horary chart cast for the moment the question comes into existence.

The horary chart is erected in the same manner as the natal chart, using the date, time and coordinates for the moment that the question is formulated. If this data is vague, the astrologer should use the date, time and coordinates for the time and place that the question is received and understood.

Horary astrology developed during a period when life was difficult and people were subjected to the whims of nature. Consequently, unlike natal interpretation, horary interpretation is subject to strict limitations, with little leeway for subjectivity.

The first and most important rule is that the person asking the question must have a valid and sincere need to obtain an answer. If this need does not exist, the chart may be confusing or contain conditions which make it unreadable.

Generally, the horary chart has an inherent time limit of approximately three months. The limitation is imposed by the nature of the question. Questions which involve changing conditions in the immediate future will be contained within this three-month limitation. The question cannot be asked again within that time period, even if it is modified to obtain a broader or more palatable answer. Questions which have a longer lasting nature are limited by the nature of the question. For example, "Will I sell my house?" is a question which has a three month time limit. The question "Will my book sell well at next year's convention?" obviously has a longer than three-month time limitation. On the other hand, subjective questions which are dependent upon psychological interpretations on the part of the individual are far too broad in scope to be answered by a horary question. For example, the question "Will my child be happily married?" is an inappropriate question. Happiness is contingent upon the value system of the individual. Additionally, life is made up of both happiness and sorrow (again reflecting the play of opposites) and one can expect one's child to have moments of happiness as well as moments of sorrow throughout life.

Aspects are important in horary astrology, as it is through analysis of aspects that the answer to the question is obtained. Only major aspects are used in the judgment of the chart. These include the conjunction, square, trine, opposition and sextile. Some astrologers place considerable importance upon the quincunx (inconjunct) and upon the parallel and contra-parallel. It is our opinion that the standard Ptolemic aspects (mentioned above) along with the quincunx are to be primarily considered. In our experience, the parallel and contra-parallel offer added support or emphasis.

Orbs are a matter of personal preference. Since the chart is future oriented, reasonably wide orbs can be considered. We generally use ten degrees for the conjunction, square, trine and opposition; seven degrees for the sextile and quincunx; and up to one and one-half degrees for the parallel and contra-parallel. However, we do prefer to remain flexible in the use of orbs and will often stretch orbs when led by the chart, especially when the Sun, Moon and Mercury are involved.

Since the horary chart questions what will happen in the future, the answer may be obtained by judging applying aspects. Separating aspects show what has already happened, and therefore lend insight to the conditions which led up to the current situation. There are some situations in which separating aspects must be considered. These are discussed later under "translation of light" and "collection of light."

The Moon is allowed the full range of all the aspects it will make while in its horary sign. Additionally, if the Moon in the horary chart is posited late in the sign, aspects formed early in the next sign are also pertinent to the horary question. In this case, after the Moon changes signs, some change may occur in the matter which may influence the question.

The person asking the question is called the **querent**. The question and the querent are both ruled by the 1st house of the horary chart. The planet which rules the sign on the 1st house is the **significator** or **ruler** of the querent and the question. Planets in the 1st house are **co-significators** or **co-rulers**.

If a sign is intercepted in the 1st house, then the planetary ruler of the intercepted sign is also a co-significator. Additionally, the Moon rules every horary question and usually co-rules the querent.

The person about whom the querent is inquiring is called the **quesited**. The astrologer should locate the house in the horary chart which normally rules that person. The planet which rules the sign on that house is the significator of the quesited. Planets in that house are co-significators, as is the planet which rules an intercepted sign in that house.

The matter about which the querent is inquiring is called the **objective**. The planet which rules the sign on the objective house is the significator of the objective. Planets in that house are co-significators, as is the planet which rules an intercepted sign in that house. The house of the objective is defined by the nature of the question. If the question involves something of the querent's, the **direct** house system is used. For example, if the querent is inquiring about employment, the tenth house from the 1st house is the **direct** objective house. (In Part IV, a **direct** house is indicated by an asterisk "*.") If the question involves something of the quesited's, then the **derivative** method is used (further explained in Part II). For example, if the querent is asking about the spouse's employment, the tenth house from the spouse-7th is the **derived** objective house (the 4th house of the horary chart).

Consider, for example, a question concerning whether or not one's child will receive an award. The 1st house would rule both the person asking the question and the question itself. The planetary ruler of the sign on the 1st house, any planets in the 1st house, the planetary ruler of any intercepted sign in the 1st house and the Moon are all significators of the question and the querent. The 5th house would rule the quesited (the child). Therefore, the planetary ruler of the sign on the 5th house, any planets in the 5th house and the planetary ruler of any intercepted sign in the 5th house are all significators of the quesited. The 2nd house of the horary chart (10th from 5th) would rule the objective (the child's award). (In this case, the objective's house is assigned through the use of the derivative house system, which is further explained in Part II.) The planetary ruler of the sign on the 2nd house, any planets in the 2nd house and the planetary ruler of any intercepted sign in the 2nd house are all significators of the objective.

Generally, trines or sextiles between the rulers of the querent and the rulers of the quesited, or in the derivative house system, between the rulers of the quesited and objective, indicate a favorable outcome to the matter. Squares, oppositions or quincunxes between the rulers indicate an unfavorable outcome to the matter. The conjunction can be read either way, but usually indicates that the two will come together. Whether the outcome is favorable or unfavorable from the standpoint of the querent must be determined through further examination of the chart. If there is no aspect between the significators, there will be no meeting of minds or no action in the matter.

There is some controversy regarding the assignment of sign rulerships for the planets beyond Saturn. Originally, the judgment of horary astrology ended with the planet Saturn. However, astrology is an ongoing, evolving science and since new planets have been discovered, we feel that these outer planets must be considered in the judgment of any horary chart. When judging the chart, if the sign has both a primary ruler and a secondary ruler, both must be considered. We use the following rulerships, the first being the primary ruler of the sign, the second being the secondary or co-ruler of the sign:

♈ ARIES	♂	Mars
♉ TAURUS	♀	Venus
♊ GEMINI	☿	Mercury
♋ CANCER	☽	Moon
♌ LEO	☉	Sun
♍ VIRGO	☿	Mercury
♎ LIBRA	♀	Venus
♏ SCORPIO	♇ ♂	Pluto, Mars
♐ SAGITTARIUS	♃ ♆	Jupiter, Neptune
♑ CAPRICORN	♄	Saturn
♒ AQUARIUS	♅ ♄	Uranus, Saturn
♓ PISCES	♆ ♃	Neptune, Jupiter

STRICTURES AGAINST JUDGMENT

There are certain conditions which may exist in the horary chart that are called **strictures against judgment**. These strictures are based upon specific rules that have been empirically employed throughout the history of horary astrology and affect the judgment of the chart even in modern times. The five traditional strictures against judgment are:

Void of Course Moon

Less than 3 degrees on the Ascendant

More than 27 degrees on the Ascendant

Saturn in the 7th house or Capricorn or Aquarius on the cusp of the 7th house.

Moon in a Via Combusta position

Void of Course Moon

A Void of Course Moon occurs when the Moon makes no major aspects (including parallel or contra-parallel, according to some sources) to any other planet before leaving its sign. In our opinion, the Moon is still Void of Course even if it aspects the Part of Fortune or an angle in the chart. No other aspects are used for determining a Void of Course Moon except those aspects previously listed. Traditionally, a Void of Course Moon indicates a stalemate situation. That is, nothing will come of the matter. Since the Moon co-rules all horary questions, the Void of Course Moon indicates that under the present circumstances nothing will function. In our experience, however, the Void of Course Moon does not render the chart unreadable. Oftentimes, if the significators of the question make strong aspects, the event will occur **beyond** the three-month time limit of the chart.

We find that the following judgments can be made in the chart with a Void of Course Moon:

1. Nothing will happen until the Moon changes sign indicating a change in circumstances.

2. The change in circumstances will change the question or render the question moot.

3. In the case of lost articles or people, the person will return or the article will be found.

4. The situation will not progress any further. Nothing will come of the matter.

5. There is no need to worry about the situation.

6. Little can be done to help or to change the situation.

7. The question is one that should not be of any concern to the querent. The querent has no valid and sincere need to obtain an answer to the question.

8. Important facts pertaining to the problem are unknown to the querent but will affect the outcome of the question.

9. The querent's interests will change, rendering the question null and void.

10. The issue is a dead-end issue. There is no answer because the issue is dead.

11. The situation is at a critical stage and almost beyond the point where any change can be effected.

If the Moon is Void of Course, but is applying by three degrees to an aspect with another planet and will perfect that aspect after changing sign, the astrologer can consider the moon as technically **not** Void of Course.

Any planet may be in a Void of Course condition and may be read in the same manner when it has some bearing upon the question, the quesited or the objective.

Less than 3 Degrees on the Ascendant

Less than 3 degrees on the Ascendant indicates that it is too early to receive an answer to the question. The question is premature because not all of the pertinent conditions have developed. Something else has to happen in the situation which will influence the outcome of the question. Oftentimes, the horary chart will indicate the area in which the querent is lacking information. Sometimes, once the new information or conditions come to light, the question is rendered obsolete.

More than 27 Degrees on the Ascendant

More than 27 degrees on the Ascendant indicates that a course of action in the matter has already been decided upon, or the querent may be asking the horary question for confirmation and support of a decision already made. In some charts, it indicates that the seeds have been sown to affect the outcome of the situation.

Traditionally, these early/late degree strictures do not apply when the querent's natal chart has the same degree on the Ascendant as the horary chart or when the horary Ascendant conjuncts a planet in the querent's natal chart. This is especially true if that planet is relevant to the question (i.e., if the question concerns real estate and the horary Ascendant conjuncts natal Saturn).

In our experience, however, neither an early nor a late degree on the Ascendant renders the chart unreadable. If the Ascendant is less than 3 degrees, oftentimes the horary chart can be examined to determine the direction in which the querent must search to obtain further clarification for the question. If the Ascendant is greater than 27 degrees, the planetary ruler of the next sign contained within the 1st house must be considered as a querent/question co-ruler. Oftentimes judging the chart in this manner sheds important additional light on the situation and can lead the querent to reevaluate the situation and choose another course of action.

Saturn in 7th/Capricorn or Aquarius on Cusp of 7th

Saturn in the 7th house or Capricorn or Aquarius on the 7th house cusp traditionally means that the astrologer does not understand the question, has made an error or cannot be objective in judging the chart. In this case, the astrologer should carefully recheck the calculations. The astrologer should also speak to the querent to ascertain that the question is thoroughly understood. Often-times, there is something about the question that makes it hard for the astrologer to judge because of some lack of communication involving the parties. Furthermore, the astrologer's degree of objectivity in judging the horary should be carefully evaluated. If the astrologer cannot be objective, the chart should be declined. When other people are involved in the outcome of the question, Saturn in the 7th house sometimes represents a delaying influence in reaching the culmination of the objective, even when the chart indicates an otherwise favorable outcome. When the astrologer is the querent, the same strictures against judgment exist if Saturn is in the 1st house or Capricorn or Aquarius is on the cusp of the 1st house.

Via Combusta Moon

The Via Combusta area is that portion of the zodiac between 15 degrees Libra and 15 degrees Scorpio. At the time the zodiac and the constellations were aligned, this segment of the sky contained a number of malefic fixed stars which seemed to debilitate or weaken any planet found in those degrees. The exception to this debilitative position is 23/24 degrees Libra, which is conjunct the benefic fixed stars Spica and Arcturus. Sometimes, when the Moon is in the Via Combusta segment of the zodiac, the normal indicators of the outcome of the horary question are contradicted and the outcome is not favorable to the querent. The circumstances take sudden, unpredictable turns and the chart operates as though it is under the influence of an eclipse. There is a connotation of an unfavorable outcome involved in the chart.

Many astrologers believe that strictures against judgment render the horary chart unreadable. However, we view these strictures as guideposts which contribute to the total interpretation of the chart and, together with other chart indicators, allow the astrologer to answer the question.

SPECIAL CONSIDERATIONS

There are other conditions which are considered weakening or debilitating factors for the horary planets. Among these are planets in the degree of the Moon's nodes and retrograde planets.

Nodal Degree

Any planet which falls in the same degree as the Moon's nodes, regardless of sign, is said to be debilitated. Some authors ascribe some form of fatality to this planet. It is our experience, however, that this placement is not necessarily fatal in the sense of life or death. Rather, the principle of the planet has an important bearing on the question, and even though the planet is not directly related to the question as a significator, the matters of the house it rules somehow are critically related. The planet in the nodal degree signifies a situation which is no longer viable; something is gone or dead. A situation is finished, as signified by the nature of the planet, its sign, and especially the house the planet rules in the horary chart. For example, a chart drawn for the question "Should I purchase a new house?" showed the ruler of the 10th house in the nodal degree. This signified that in some way the career of the querent was debilitated or in danger of being terminated. Even when the chart showed a positive answer concerning the purchase of the new home, the querent's career situation had to be considered before he assumed the additional financial obligation. Ignorance of the potentially fatal career situation would have had an adverse impact upon his decision to purchase the new home. However, prior knowledge of the career situation prompted the querent to take steps to protect his career and limit the fatal connotation of the chart.

Retrograde Planets

Retrograde planets have special meaning in the horary chart. Any significator which is retrograde is considered to be debilitated or weakened. A debilitated or weakened significator does not necessarily mean that the outcome will be unfavorable. Oftentimes a retrograde planet can have a positive connotation.

If the querent's aspects are positively configured with the ruler of the objective and either ruler is retrograde, the querent may achieve the objective, but the objective may turn out to be undesirable or disadvantageous. The querent is well advised to postpone any action until after the retrograde planet(s) turn direct. If the question concerns a pending agreement between two parties (sale of property, marriage, etc.), and either significator is retrograde, then the party whose significator is retrograde will probably have a change of mind. If the retrograde planet is the significator of a lost child, pet or article, that person will return or that thing will be found. However, the condition of the lost person or thing can be debilitated.

Retrograde planets can also mean returning to a former condition. For example, if the question concerns finding employment and the ruler of the 10th house is retrograde, the querent will find it advantageous to return to a former position. If the question concerns marriage, separation or divorce and the significator of the 1st or the 7th is retrograde, the person represented by the retrograde planet will have a change of heart.

Oftentimes, if the ruler of the quesited is retrograde, that person may be unavailable or inaccessible to the querent or difficult to reach.

Some astrologers feel that retrograde Mercury affects the entire question even though it is not involved as a significator in the chart. In this case, the querent or quesited may have a change of mind or the conditions surrounding the matter may be altered.

Mutual Reception

Mutual reception is a strengthening factor in the horary chart and occurs when any two planets in the chart are located in each other's signs. For example, Venus in Gemini and Mercury in Taurus are in mutual reception. A mutual reception in the horary chart allows the planet to be read as though it occupies its own sign in the same degree placement as the mutual reception planet, as well as occupying its actual placement in the chart. It is read first as having its own aspects and second as having the aspects of the planet in mutual reception.

Translation of Light

Translation of light is one of two circumstances under which the horary question can be answered based upon separating aspects. It occurs when two significators are separating from an aspect to each other (or actually make **no** aspect to each other), and a third **faster moving** planet aspects first one of the significators and immediately the other, before changing sign or before making any aspect to another planet. This third planet **translates the light** from one significator to the other, thereby reactivating the separating aspect. It is through a third party, represented by the faster moving planet, or through conditions existing prior to the horary question that the matter is brought to fruition. This conclusion may be either favorable or unfavorable, depending upon the aspects between the significators as well as the aspect made by the planet translating the light. For example, if Saturn is at 2 ♍ and Mars is at 7 ♉ (both significators and separating from a trine), and the Sun at 1 ♑ first trines Saturn and then trines the Mars, the Sun would "translate the light" of the trine between Saturn and the Mars thereby reinstating the contact. Another example: the Moon at 8 ♊ will sextile first the significator Jupiter at 10 ♈ and then the significator Mars at 12 ♌. The Moon will "translate the light" by reinforcing the separating trine between the two significators.

Collection of Light

Collection of light is another circumstance under which the horary question can be read based upon separating aspects. Collection of light occurs when two significators are separating from an aspect to each other, but both are applying in aspect to a third **slower moving** planet. This third planet represents a third party to whom the others can turn who will be helpful in bringing the matter to a conclusion. Again, whether the conclusion is favorable or unfavorable depends upon the separating aspect between the two significators, and the aspects they make to the slower planet. For example, if Mars at 5 ♈ and the Sun at 7 ♎ are the significators in the chart, and both are applying to a square to Saturn at 9 ♋, Saturn would "collect the light" from the Sun (when the Sun makes its aspect to Saturn) and bring it to Mars (when Mars makes its aspect to Saturn) allowing the separating opposition between the two significators to be read as an applying opposition. Another example: Venus at 4 ♉ and the Moon at 9 ♍ are significators in the chart. Saturn at 11 ♏ would "collect the light" from the Moon and bring it to Venus, allowing the separating trine between Venus and the Moon to be read as an applying trine.

It should be noted that when reference is made to the speed of a planet, we are referring to that planet's rate of motion through the zodiac. The rate of motion is determined by the planet's distance from the Sun. The closer the planet is to the Sun, the faster its orbit around the Sun and the faster its movement through the zodiac. The planetary movement, starting with the fastest moving planets and progressing to the slowest is as follows:

Moon	☽
Mercury	☿
Venus	♀
Sun	☉
Mars	♂
Jupiter	♃
Saturn	♄
Uranus	♅
Neptune	♆
Pluto	♇

While most of the time Pluto is slower in motion than Neptune, at the present time and through the turn of the century, Pluto's orbit is closer to the Sun than Neptune's. Therefore, Neptune's rate of motion through the zodiac is slower than Pluto's. Consequently, at the present time we view Neptune's speed as the slowest in the zodiac.

Refranation

The condition of **refranation** exists when two significators are applying to an aspect to each other, but before completing the aspect, one of the two turns retrograde. The individual signified by the planet which turns retrograde will probably back out of the matter or have a change of mind.

THE NATAL CHART

The horary chart is a valid tool and can be read independently of any other astrological chart. However, whenever possible, the astrologer should examine the querent's natal chart along with the horary chart. If the querent's natal chart has the same degree on the Ascendant as the horary chart, the question is considered extremely important. If the horary Ascendant conjuncts a planet in the querent's natal chart, that planet is extremely important and is read as being a querent/question secondary co-ruler. It is our opinion that traditional horary rulerships take precedence and while it is important to examine the relationship of the natal planets to the horary, the answer is still in the horary.

OTHER BRANCHES OF ASTROLOGY

There are several branches of astrology which have a close relationship to horary astrology. Two of these are **event** astrology and **electional** astrology. Event astrology involves the casting of a chart for the time and place of an event which has already taken place. These charts are read in the same manner as horary charts. However, the strictures against judgment may be ignored and both applying and separating aspects are used. Electional astrology charts are cast for a predetermined time for future events. In this case, the astrologer selects a time in the future to initiate an event which will have a **birth chart** with favorable indicators. If the event is in fact initiated at that preselected moment, that chart is the event chart for that happening. Again, this chart is read in the same manner as horary charts, but the strictures against judgment are ignored and both applying and separating aspects are used. Furthermore, when using electional charts, the astrologer **must** take into consideration the initiator's natal and progressed configurations.

PART II

CONTROVERSIAL AREAS

UNIVERSAL RELATIONSHIPS, DERIVATIVES AND STEPPING

In horary astrology, one can expect a valid answer to a question only when there is a valid and sincere need to obtain an answer. If no valid relationship exists, the chart often will contain a stricture against judgment or the chart will be confusing and unreadable.

The Derivative House System

The derivative house system is simply a method by which the astrologer turns the chart and uses another house as the 1st house. For example, if the querent is asking about a spouse, the querent is represented by the 1st house and the spouse is represented by the 7th house. This is a **direct** house. In counting derivative houses, one counts the quesited's house as the 1st house and counts houses from there. For example, if the querent is asking about the spouse's employer, the chart is turned to use the 7th house as the 1st, and the employer is represented by the 10th house from the 7th (the 4th house of the horary chart). This is a **derived** house since, within the context of the question, the querent has no relationship to the employer except through the spouse.

This method of obtaining derivative houses can be extended into further derivatives. For example, the querent's mother is represented by the 10th house, a direct house, since the mother has a **direct** relationship to the querent. However, the house used for the querent's maternal aunt (the mother's sister) is a 1st derivative house and is obtained by locating the 3rd (sibling) house from the 10th (mother) house. Therefore, the maternal aunt is represented in the chart by the 12th house. One could even go further. For example, if the querent were asking about a first cousin on the mother's side, the astrologer would seek out the second derivative by locating the maternal aunt's house and then, beginning with the maternal aunt's house as the 1st house, counting five houses to obtain that aunt's child's house (the querent's cousin). This would be the 4th house of the horary chart (the second derivative).

The reader must understand that in **all** cases, one must use the derivative house which has the **closest** relationship to the querent. Otherwise, the entire derivative house system breaks down. For example, if the querent is asking about a child, rather than look at the 5th house from the 7th (the spouse's child) or seeking the child's house as the grandchild of the querent's mother, the astrologer **must** use the 5th house. The closest relationship the child has to the querent is as the querent's child.

In the event the querent is asking about a stepchild, the relationship of the child to the querent is **through** the spouse. In this case, one must use the first derivative by locating the 5th house (child) from the 7th (spouse) or the 11th house of the horary chart.

A godchild falls in the 11th house (5th from 7th), as the godchild is the child of another person. If the godchild has another relationship to the querent such as a niece or nephew, then the astrologer must use the closest and most direct relationship to the querent. In this case the relationship of niece or nephew is most direct.

Whenever there is a question as to what approach to take in determining the proper house to use, the astrologer will be most correct by following the most logical and direct avenue.

While the 1st house represents the querent, sometimes, when using the derivative house system, it will also represent either the quesited or the objective. In this case, the planetary ruler of the 1st house and planets posited therein should be used as significators of the quesited or objective and the Moon should be used as the significator of the querent and question.

Stepping

Although the term ''stepping'' has not been used before, we use it here to differentiate between the selection of derivative houses and the selection of houses used in multiple-subject questions. There are several different methods of stepping and there is much confusion about which method is correct. The techniques used to obtain the derivative houses can be extended when questions are asked about multiple subjects which are alike in nature and which all have the same relationship to the querent (i.e., two cars, two friends, two children). Through the study of many horary charts, we began to realize that there **does** seem to be some cosmic order involved in the selection of houses for multiple-subject questions. The selection of the proper houses is accomplished by analyzing the relationship of the querent to the quesited, and of the quesited to the quesited and then using one of two stepping methods. It should be noted here that many astrologers prefer not to interpret multiple-question charts, and will encourage their clients to ask the questions individually and at different times.

The first method is used **only** when a blood relationship exists between the quesited and the quesited. When using this method, the second quesited is assigned to a house based upon the actual relationship between the two.

For example, a question concerning two or more children of the same querent/parent is dealt with by assigning the 5th house (children) to the first child. Then, step to the 3rd house from the 5th house (sibling blood relationship to first child), or the 7th house of the horary chart, and assign it to the second child. If a third child is included in the same horary question, the 3rd house from the 7th must be used for the third child (the 3rd from the 3rd from the 5th), or the 9th house of the horary chart. Another example can be seen when the question concerns more than one of the querent's siblings. The first sibling would be the 3rd house and the second sibling would be the 5th house (3rd from 3rd), since the relationship between the two siblings is also a sibling (3rd house) blood relationship. This principle can also be extended by using both the derivative system and the stepping system simultaneously. Suppose that the querent asks a question about two maternal aunts. Here, the astrologer would first locate the querent's mother's house in the chart (10th). Then the first maternal aunt would be the 3rd from the 10th (the 12th house of the horary chart). The second maternal aunt would be represented by the horary 2nd house (3rd from 12th).

The second method of stepping is used for **both** animate and inanimate items, as long as there exists a "need to know" for the querent and there is no blood relationship between the two quesiteds. This method is used for objects, possessions, pets, and any other living things except adopted children, ex-spouses or other "ex" relationships. (These will be discussed separately.) When using this method, the second quesited is assigned to a house the same number of houses away from the first as the first is away from the querent's house. For example, the first automobile would be assigned the 3rd house, the second automobile would be assigned the 5th house (the 3rd from 3rd). If a question concerns a choice between the querent's present home and a future home, or the choice between purchasing one home or another, the first home is signified by the 4th house, the second home is signified by the 7th house of the horary chart (4th from 4th). If the question concerns a choice between two pets, the first pet would be the 6th house and the second pet would be the 11th house of the horary chart (the 6th from the 6th).

There appear to be two exceptions to these rules. The first concerns adopted children, who in reality have no blood relationship to either their adopted parents or their adopted siblings. However, the legal and moral relationship between the parents and the adopted child is no different than the relationship between the same parents and their biological children. The relationship between the adopted child and its adopted parents should be **assumed** to be a blood relationship, and the adopted child is still signified by the 5th house. Furthermore, the relationship between the adopted child and its adopted siblings should **also** be assumed to be a blood relationship. Therefore, if the querent is the mother and the question concerns two of her children, one of whom is adopted and one of whom is her biological child, the first quesited child is ruled by the 5th house and the second quesited child is ruled by the 7th house (3rd from 5th). The same would apply if both the children are adopted.

The second exception to the above rule concerns ex-spouses. The first method is to analyze the relationship of the querent to the ex-spouse according to the question. If the ex-spouse is still a friend, then that individual would be assigned the 11th house. If the ex-spouse is a secret enemy, then the assignment would be the 12th house. If the ex-spouse is related to the querent as an employer, then the 10th house would be used. If the ex-spouse is the parent of the querent's child, then the closest relationship to the querent is through the child and the house would be located by using the first derivative house (the 4th from the 5th if the parent is the father, the 10th from the 5th if the parent is the mother). When the ex-spouse has a dual relationship to the querent (i.e., employer as well as parent of the querent's child), then the closest relationship to the querent is dependent upon the nature of the question. If the question concerns something about the employment, the closest relationship to the ex-spouse would be as employer and the 10th house would be used. In the event that the question concerns something about the relationship to the child (child support payments, etc.), the closest relationship would be as parent of the child. Then, the horary 8th house (4th from child-5th) would be used if the individual is the child's father and the horary 2nd house (10th from child-5th) would be used if the individual is the child's mother. However, if the ex-spouse has **no** other relationship to the querent and there are no children involved, then any question regarding that individual could violate the first cardinal rule of horary astrology since there may be no valid and sincere relationship between the querent and the quesited. Perhaps the question should not be asked.

This principle is extended to any "ex" relationship. For example, a question about an "ex" sister-in-law (brother's ex-wife) must be approached through the second derivative if there are children from the marriage. In this case, the astrologer would use the 3rd house as the brother's house, then step to the fifth from the 3rd (the horary 7th) for the house of the nieces/nephews, and then examine the 10th from the 7th (the horary 4th) for their mother (the querent's ex-sister-in-law). On the other hand, if there are no children from the marriage, then the astrologer must examine the querent's relationship to the quesited. Does a valid relationship exist between the querent and the "ex"? If so, the nature of the relationship would determine the house to use in the horary chart.

Many astrologers prefer to use a different method when answering questions about ex-spouses. One method is to use the nonblood relationship rule, assigning the current spouse to the 7th house, assigning the first ex-spouse inquired about to the 1st house (7th from 7th), then assigning the Moon to the querent. If the Moon favorably aspects the significator of the 7th, the outcome for the current spouse is favored. If the Moon favorably aspects the significator of the 1st, the outcome for the ex-spouse is favored. This method, however, breaks down when inquiring about more than one ex-spouse, since the second ex-spouse would be also assigned to the 7th house. A second method used by some astrologers assigns the current spouse to the 7th house, the first ex-spouse to the 9th, the second ex-spouse to the 11th, etc. While we do not agree with these methods, the reader is invited to experiment with them in order to test their validity. We would appreciate your comments and opinions.

MOTHER/FATHER

One of the biggest controversial areas in both natal and horary astrology is the assignment of the houses ruling the mother and the father. Traditionally, horary astrology assigns the 10th house to the mother and the 4th house to the father. However, many popular sources grant the 10th house to the father and the 4th house to the mother. This is an important issue in the practice of horary astrology, as the proper selection of the derivative house is dependent upon the proper selection of the direct house.

Sylvia De Long generally accepts the traditional assignment of the mother in the 10th. However, she states that this doesn't always work out in actual practice. "If the querent has only one living parent, use the 10th house for the quesited, whether mother or father, as this house represents the remaining authority symbol."[1] De Long suggests an alternate method by which one studies the signs of the 4th and 10th houses to see which best fits the parent in question.[2]

Margaret E. Hone also indicates that the chart must be studied to see which house best fits the parent in question. She says "This house [4th] generally refers to the mother, though the connection is not infallible as older books imply."[3] She continues, "Its [the 10th house's] connection with the father is by no means infallible, though the fourth and tenth houses may show the parent from the angle of vision of the child in question."[4]

Nicholas de Vore summarizes several different opinions. One method is to use the traditional assignments for a daytime birth, and the opposite (father in the 10th, mother in the 4th) for a nighttime birth.[5] No further explanation is given, however, of what constitutes "day-births" and "night-births." Does one use 6:00 AM, or does one use the actual time of sunrise/sunset? A second method is to use the 10th house for the parent of the same sex as the individual, and the 4th house for the parent of the opposite sex.[6] Sepharial suggest these same rulerships.[7] A third method discussed by de Vore assigns the 10th house to the father of a female or to the mother of a male.[8] These methods seem to break down in horary Astrology, as they

1. Sylvia De Long, *The Art of Horary Astrology in Practice* (Tempe, Arizona: American Federation of Astrologers, Inc.), p. 22.
2. Ibid.
3. Margaret E. Hone, *The Modern Textbook of Astrology* (London, England: L.N. Fowler & Co., Ltd., 1951), p. 93.
4. Hone, p. 95.
5. Nicholas de Vore, *Encyclopedia of Astrology* (Totowa, New Jersey: Littlefield, Adams & Co., 1976), p. 211.
6. Ibid.
7. Sepharial, *The Manual of Astrology* (New York, NY.: Wholesale Book Corp., 1972), p. 28.
8. de Vore, p. 211.

assign the same house to both the querent's parent and the querent's in-law of the same sex as that parent.

A fourth method uses the Hindu allocations of mother in the 4th and father in the 10th.[9] We believe that this is based on the natural zodiacal rulerships of the sign Cancer for the 4th representing the womb and Capricorn for the 10th representing the conservative, restricting qualities of the father in a patriarchal society. A fifth method requires the determination of which parent is the more authoritative parent to the individual.[10] Although it is not stated in de Vore's book, one can assume that this method might assign the authoritative parent to the 10th house. This same "authoritative parent in the 10th" theory is suggested by Heindel.[11]

Liz Greene states:

> To some significant extent, however, they [10th house to mother, 4th to father rulerships] have proved valid, and they therefore warrant consideration. The relationship with the father seems to be reflected most clearly by the north point of the chart (the IC) and by any planets which fall in the fourth house. The relationship with the mother seems to be reflected most clearly by the midheaven, the south point (the MC) and by any planets which fall in the tenth house.[12]

Raphael assigns the 4th to father and the 10th to the mother.[13] Moore and Douglas attribute the 4th to the mother and the 10th to the father.[14] Geraldine Davis gives the 4th house to the mother **or** father, and the 10th to the mother-in-law **or** father-in-law.[15] Barbara Watters gives the 10th house to the mother.[16] Llewellyn George states:

> Reference to twelve of the leading astrological textbooks, published during the past three hundred years, shows the tenth house ruling the mother; fourth house, the father. Only one of the early writers reverses this indication, while another, who leans toward Eastern methods quotes the tenth house as ruling father in the horoscope of females, mother in male charts; the fourth ruling mother in the horoscope of females, the father in male charts. My own experience confirms the teachings of the twelve older writers. It is an invariable rule in Horary Astrology to use the tenth house for mother and fourth for father in all cases.[17]

It is our opinion and experience that while the parents, as a unit, may be viewed from the 4th house of the natal chart, and the parent-in-laws, as a whole, may be viewed from the 10th house, the traditional **horary** rulership

---

9. Ibid.
10. Ibid.
11. Max Heindel and Augusta Foss, *The Message of the Stars* (London, England: L.N. Fowler & Co., Ltd., 1973), p. 17.
12. Liz Greene, *Relating* (New York: Samuel Wiser, Inc.), p. 202.
13. Raphael, *Raphael's Horary Astrology* (London, England: W. Foulsham & Co., 1897), pp. 25-28.
14. Marcia Moore and Mark Douglas, *Astrology, The Divine Science* (York Harbor, Maine: Arcane Publications), pp. 313, 337.
15. Geraldine Davis, *A Modern Scientific Textbook on Horary Astrology* (Los Angeles, California: First Temple of Astrology, 1942), p. 92, 102.
16. Barbara H. Watters, *Horary Astrology and the Judgment of Events* (Washington, D.C.: Valhalla Paperbacks, Ltd., 1973), p. 67.
17. Llewellyn George, *A to Z Horoscope Maker and Delineator* (St. Paul, Minnesota: Llewellyn Publications, 1974), p. 34.

is indeed valid. The planetary ruler of the 10th house is the significator for the mother and the planetary ruler of the 4th house is the significator for the father. These assignments have truly stood the test of time and deserve to be carried forward into the twenty-first century.

SCHOOLS AND TEACHERS

Traditionally, horary astrology assigns the rulership of elementary schools to the 3rd house and the rulership of colleges and universities to the 9th house. Many astrologers prefer to assign the 3rd house to elementary schools and the 5th house (3rd from 3rd) to high schools. In this country the school system is slowly evolving into a four-level system consisting of elementary school, middle school or junior high school, high school, and college or university. The selection of the proper house depends upon the kind of school in which the individual is enrolled. If a child is in the same school from first grade through twelfth grade, then the entire school experience can be read in the 3rd house. If, however, that child attends a different school for the high school years, then the elementary school is the 3rd house and the high school is the 5th house (3rd from 3rd). If the child attends an elementary school, then a middle or junior high school, and finally a high school, then the elementary school is the 3rd house, the middle school is the 5th house (3rd from 3rd), and the high school is the 7th house (3rd from 5th).

The school issue is further complicated by a new line of reasoning which classifies today's undergraduate colleges on the same level as high schools and assigns only graduate school to the 9th house. However, in our opinion, the entire college experience is a 9th house matter. Furthermore, the stepping system seems to confirm the three level precollege school system prevalent in this country today.

Most trade schools seem to fall into the same category as high schools. The exceptions to this are the trade schools which require a high school diploma as an entrance prerequisite. These are assigned to the 9th house.

Apprenticeship programs, by their very nature, are assigned to the 6th house, as these are programs through which the individual works in a craft or trade and is financially remunerated while learning the trade.

Special education and handicapped programs are learning experiences designed to teach the individual to cope with the immediate environment. Therefore, they have a 3rd house assignment.

In natal astrology, a teacher could be classified according to the educational level taught. For example, the teacher in a special education program may be assigned a 3rd house rulership. The university professor, who is responsible for contributing to the philosophical mind expansion of students, may be ruled by the 9th house. However, in horary astrology, teachers are signified by the 3rd house, regardless of the educational level taught.

AUTOMOBILES

Any means used to explore one's immediate surroundings or neighborhood would be assigned to the 3rd house, the traditional ruler of short-distance transportation. The 3rd house includes all vehicles of transportation used for this exploration. By extension, the 3rd house is assigned the rulership of automobiles, even though automobiles are sometimes used for distant trips.

Robert De Luce uses the 4th house of the chart for vehicles, "since it is the 2nd house from the 3rd, i.e., the means or tools of locomotion."[18] We question this assignment. In every reference we checked the means of transportation (wagons, bicycles, trains, etc.) were assigned to the 3rd house. This is the most logical, since the vehicle has a direct relationship to the querent, and should not be assigned a secondary or derivative position. It has been our experience that the 3rd house signifies automobiles.

ANCESTORS

In all the traditional astrology books, ancestors are given to the 2nd house. The only logic we find for this assignment is that the derivative house system is used and the 2nd house is the 12th house (the distant past) from the 3rd house (relatives). It is our feeling that the 4th house possibly has more bearing on ancestors than the 2nd. The 4th house represents the general circumstances of one's foundations and private life. It represents the heritage, which is one's primary foundation. It concerns matters or people of the past which include the members of the family tree. The 12th house, on the other hand, represents the past in terms of archetypes and racial memories. It is true that these are also part of our heritage, but this is in a more impersonal, unrelated sense. The heritage of the 4th house is more direct and encompasses all that comes to us through our genetic imprint. Therefore, we have chosen to list the 4th house for ancestors in this volume.

PETS

Traditionally, pets are assigned a 6th house rulership. The 6th house is the house of debts, obligations and maintenance, and certainly, when one accepts the responsibility for a pet, one has the obligation to properly feed and care for that pet. Some astrologers assign a 5th house rulership to those pets which are cared for, pampered and loved as one would a child. We disagree with this assignment. Regardless of how close one is to one's pet, the relationship is never equal to the relationship of a parent to a child. Inherent in the Leo/Sun/5th house principle is the connotation of immortality, perpetuated through one's children. A pet is not the product of one's own

18. Robert De Luce, *Horary Astrology* (New York: ASI Publications, Inc., 1932), p. 81.

creativity. Nor does the ownership of a pet satisfy the archetypal urge for immortality in humans.

Other animals, either large or wild, are traditionally assigned 12th house rulership. There is, however, some confusion in this area, as one can have a very large horse which is a pet, yet traditional astrology tells us that the horse is assigned to the 12th house. Primarily the 12th house represents some sort of contact with another realm. It represents the collective unconscious that impinges itself on the individual through latent archetypal urges which we call instinct. We as humans are very much unaware of these instinctive urges. However, animals in the wild respond almost solely upon and survive by these very instincts.

It is our opinion that these different principles of the 6th/12th houses **must** be considered when assigning animal rulerships in the horary chart. Any animal for which humans must assume direct obligation and responsibility for its care and feeding **must** be assigned to the 6th house, since the domestication of the animal diminished its instinctual survival urges. Any animal which sustains itself in the wild **must** be assigned to the 12th house. For example, a horse, regardless of whether or not it is considered a pet, would be assigned to the 6th house if it must be periodically fed and cared for. If it is left to its own devices to roam the range and fend for itself, it then would be assigned to the 12th house. Cattle kept on breeding farms, in dairies, etc., which must be attended to, are 6th house. Cattle left to fatten on large ranches and never cared for until roundup time are 12th house.

Wild animals in zoos are 6th house. They must be cared for on a daily basis, fed, and provided with veterinarian services. We have assumed the responsibility for all these things by virtue of the fact that we have confined them. We have the obligation to see to their care and maintenance. Therefore, they are 6th house. Wild animals in their own natural habitat, those to which we never give a second thought, those which rely on their own instincts to provide their own food and shelter, those which are at the mercy of nature, are 12th house.

As with other animals, dogs can be either 6th house or 12th house. For example, the neighborhood dog that bites you belongs to someone. Someone is responsible for it; the owner can be held legally accountable. Therefore, that dog is assigned a 6th house rulership. However, the dog that has no owner, the one which is the scavenger, the wild dog which depends upon its own instincts for survival, is assigned to the 12th house.

When considering house rulerships for animals in the horary chart, the astrologer must evaluate whether or not people are responsible and accountable for the animal, or whether the animal survives in the wild relying on its own instincts.

THE STOCK EXCHANGE
AND THE STOCK MARKET

Traditional astrology assigns the stock exchange to the 11th house. The 11th house has rulership over groups of people who band together for a common cause. The stock exchange is composed of membership corporations which come together to trade. While it is true that this organization also invests, earns money, and pays salaries and expenses, its primary purpose is to provide a marketplace in which member corporations can trade. Stock exchanges can be incorporated or can be composed of voluntary membership. In the United States, the exchanges are composed of voluntary membership. An exchange might be incorporated and although corporations are normally given to the 9th house in horary astrology, this does not affect the 11th house assignment for the stock exchange.

There seems to be much controversy about the house rulership for stocks and bonds. Some authors assign the 2nd house to preferred stocks and the 5th house to common stocks. In some references the 3rd house is mentioned. In order to assign the proper house, one must examine the nature of stocks and bonds.

A stock certificate is evidence of a small piece of ownership in a corporation. Once a corporation decides to issue shares of stock, these shares are turned over to a member of the stock exchange for sale. After the initial sale, the stock can continue to be traded on the stock exchange, but the issuing company is not involved in the trade, nor does it receive any additional money. People purchase stock with the idea of securing a profit on the investment. It is always speculative, and **never** is the profit guaranteed. Therefore, the purchase is an investment and because of the constant speculative nature, stocks belong in the 5th house.

The same thing holds true for bonds. A bond is a certificate that represents a loan to a corporation. Oftentimes, to raise working capital, a corporation will authorize the issuance of bonds. These bonds are sold on the stock exchange. The corporation promises to repay the loan at a specified rate of interest. As the open market interest rates fluctuate, investors purchase these bonds from other investors with the idea of profiting from the interest rate fluctuations. In a rapidly changing market, bonds can be highly speculative. While it is true that the bonds represent loans and must be paid off, if the issuing corporation goes bankrupt, its assets are sold to pay off the outstanding debts, including bonds. In many cases, these assets may not completely cover the bonds and the bonds are then paid off at a reduced value. Again, this emphasizes the speculative nature of bonds and supports the 5th house assignment. Even if an individual invests in a "sure thing," profit is never guaranteed, and that individual always takes some sort of financial risk. Anything of a speculative nature such as this must be assigned to the 5th house. Anytime there is some element of a gamble, it is a 5th house matter. Again, we encourage the reader to experiment with this and we are open to comments.

COURT CASES AND LAWSUITS

In any court case, lawsuit, or legal arbitration, the querent is signified by the 1st house. In the direct horary chart, one in which the question concerns the querent's own case, the planetary ruler of the sign on the 1st house is the significator of the querent and the question, along with the Moon and any planets posited in the 1st house. This is true regardless of whether the querent is the plaintiff or the defendant. The querent's adversary is always represented by the 7th house. The 10th house of the chart represents the final authority in the case: the arbitrator or the judge. The judge is also represented by Jupiter. The 4th house represents the verdict or the outcome of the case.

Lawyers are represented by both the 7th house and the 9th house. The 7th house signifies the lawyer in all situations where legal advice, counsel and services are rendered. However, when the lawyer represents the querent in a legal action before a court of law, that lawyer is signified by the 9th house.

The lawsuit itself, as an action in a court of law, is also represented by the 9th house. The jury is represented by the 11th house.

The 2nd house indicates the resources of the querent, and the 8th house represents the resources of the querent's adversary. The 3rd house signifies all the witnesses involved in the case, regardless of whether they are testifying for the querent or the adversary. The 12th house indicates the adversary's hidden motives.

In criminal cases, Saturn represents the police and Mercury represents the evidence, including alibis.

The rules for the derivative house system and stepping are applicable here. For example, if the querent asks a question regarding a lawsuit filed by the spouse, the 1st house would represent the querent and the 7th house would represent the spouse, regardless of whether the spouse is the plaintiff or the defendant. In this case, the 4th house (10th from spouse-7th) would signify the judge, the 5th house (11th from spouse-7th) would signify the jury, and the 10th house (4th from spouse-7th) would represent the outcome of the case.

REAL ESTATE

Many contemporary horary astrologers disagree on house assignments for questions concerning the purchase and sale of property. Some astrologers feel that an invariable rulership applies which assigns the 1st house to the buyer, the 7th house to the seller, the 4th house to the property, and the 10th house to the price of the property.

Other astrologers use a more flexible assignment, giving the 1st house to the querent, regardless of whether the querent is the buyer or the seller. Our experience indicates that this is a more rational method. The property in question is always the 4th house and the other party in the transaction is the 7th house. The value of the property to the querent is indicated by the 4th house, as is the condition of the property. The value of the property to the other party is indicated by the 10th house. The actual selling price is negotiated as some form of compromise between these two values. The 2nd house represents the querent's financial resources and the 8th house represents the other party's financial resources.

As in all horary charts, the derivative house system is applicable. For example, if the inquiry is about property being purchased or sold by the querent's grown child, the 5th would represent the child, the 8th would represent the property, and the 11th would represent the other party in the transaction.

PART III

BASIC OUTLINE
FOR HORARY ASTROLOGY

BASIC OUTLINE

The following outline is provided as a guide for the horary astrologer to use in the interpretation of the horary chart. The reader will note that all these points are covered in the interpretation of the example charts in Part VIII. The astrologer need not follow this outline verbatim, but rather use it as a checklist to make sure important conditions are not overlooked.

1. Make sure the question is understood. Discuss the matter with the querent to ascertain that there are no hidden questions within the spoken question.
2. Note the full data for the time the question is received (day, month, year, time, latitude and longitude). If the question is telephoned to the astrologer (even if it is a long distance call), use the time and place for where the astrologer is located and understands the question. If the question is written in a letter and the letter includes the data, use that data. Otherwise, use the time and place for where the astrologer reads and understands the question.
3. Be sure that the querent has a right and a need to know the answer to the question. If not, the astrologer should decline to do the reading.
4. Calculate the chart. Traditionally, horary astrologers have used the Tropical/Placidus method of chart erection.
5. Utilize *The Horary Reference Book* to establish the appropriate houses for the quesited (if any) and the objective.
6. Identify the significators of the quesited (if any) and the objective.
7. Calculate all appropriate aspects normally used in horary astrology. (See Part I of *The Horary Reference Book*.) Include all the Moon's aspects until it changes sign.
8. Note aspects involving translation of light, collection of light or refranation. Also note retrograde planets.
9. Examine the chart for conditions which indicate strictures against judgment. Note these.
10. Examine the chart for planets in mutual reception, Via Combusta, or nodal degree. Note these.

Take command! Do not be afraid to judge the chart.

11. Interpret the chart by analyzing the aspects between the querent and the objective, or the quesited and the objective. Renumber houses if necessary.
12. Balance the aspects made between important significators to the question and other conditions existing in the chart (strictures, retrograde condition, etc.). The answer to the question lies in the aspects made between important significators. Strictures and other chart conditions clarify that answer in some way. The astrologer must judge whether this balance leans towards a favorable outcome to the question or an unfavorable outcome. Herein lies the art of horary astrology.

PART IV

HOUSE RULERSHIPS
ALPHABETICAL LISTING

Subject	House	Derivation
A		
Abbeys	12	
Abortion (spontaneous)	5	*
Abortion (surgical)	8	*
Academies	*	See "Schools"
Accidents to Querent	1	*
Accountants	8	*
Accounts	8	*
Achievements	10	*
Acquaintances	11	*
Acting	5	*
Acupuncture (practitioners of)	6	*
Administration	10	*
Administrators	10	*
Adopted Brothers/Sisters	3	*
Adopted Child	5	See "Child (adopted)"
Adultery	5	*
Adventures	5	*
Adversaries (legal or otherwise)	7	*
Advertising	3	*
Advertising Agencies	9	*
Advertisers	3	*
Advisors	7	*
Agents	3	*
Agents (travel)	9	*
Agents (welfare)	6	(7th from welfare-12th)
Agreements	7	*
Agreements (written)	3	*
Aggressor (in war)	1	*
Agriculture	4	*
Air Force	6	See "Armed Services"
Air Mail	3	*
Aircraft	9	*
Airline Steward/Stewardess	9	*
Airports	9	*
Alderman	11	*
Alias	1	*
Aliens	9	*
Alimony	8	*
Allergies	6	*
Ambassadors (from other countries)	5	*

Subject	House	Derivation
Ambassadors (to other countries)	11	*
Ambulances	3	*
Ambushes	12	*
Ammunition	8	(2nd from war-7th)
Amusement Areas	5	*
Amusements	5	*
Ancestors	4	*
Ancients	12	*
Animal Husbandry	6	*
Animals (domestic)	6	*
Animals (large, domestic)	6	*
Animals (large, wild)	12	*
Animals (small, domestic)	6	*
Animals (small, wild)	12	*
Animals (wild)	12	*
Annulments	7	*
Anonymous Letters	3	*
Antibiotics	6	*
Antiques	4	*
Arbitrator	7	*
Arcade Games	5	*
Archbishops	9	*
Archives	6	*
Archivists	6	*
Arenas	5	*
Armed Services	6	*
Arms (artificial)	6	*
Army	6	See "Armed Services"
Art (works of) (as a possession)	2	*
Art (works of) (as an investment)	5	*
Artifacts	4	*
Artificial Arms	6	*
Artificial Breast	6	*
Artificial Eyes	6	*
Artificial Feet	6	*
Artificial Hands	6	*
Artificial Insemination	5	*
Artificial Legs	6	*
Ashrams	12	*
Assassination	12	*
Assassins	12	*
Assembly Line	6	*

Subject	House	Derivation
Associations (fraternal)	11	*
Astral Entities	12	*
Astral Travel	9	*
Astrologer (as querent)	1	*
Astrologer (for querent)	7	*
Astrology	9	*
Asylums	12	*
Atlas	3	*
Atomic Weapons	8	(2nd from war-7th)
Attacker	12	*
Attorneys	*	See "Lawyers"
Auctions	10	*
Audiences	7	*
Audit	8	*
Aunt/Uncle (maternal)	12	(3rd from mother-10th)
Aunt's/Uncle's (maternal) confinement	11	(12th from aunt/uncle-12th)
Aunt's/Uncle's (maternal) career	9	(10th from aunt/uncle-12th)
Aunt's/Uncle's (maternal) co-workers	5	(6th from aunt/uncle-12th)
Aunt's/Uncle's (maternal) death	7	(8th from aunt/uncle-12th)
Aunt's/Uncle's (maternal) employees	5	(6th from aunt/uncle-12th)
Aunt's/Uncle's (maternal) employer	9	(10th from aunt/uncle-12th)
Aunt's/Uncle's (maternal) father-in-law	9	(4th from aunt/uncle spouse-6th)
Aunt's/Uncle's (maternal) friends	10	(11th from aunt/uncle-12th)
Aunt's/Uncle's (maternal) health/illness	5	(6th from aunt/uncle-12th)
Aunt's/Uncle's (maternal) hospitalization	11	(12th from aunt/uncle-12th)
Aunt's/Uncle's (maternal) inheritance	7	(8th from aunt/uncle-12th)
Aunt's/Uncle's (maternal) mother-in-law	3	(10th from aunt/uncle-spouse-6th)
Aunt's/Uncle's (maternal) neighbors	2	(3rd from aunt/uncle-12th)
Aunt's/Uncle's (maternal) open enemies	6	(7th from aunt/uncle-12th)
Aunt's/Uncle's (maternal) partner	6	(7th from aunt/uncle-12th)
Aunt's/Uncle's (maternal) physical condition	12	*
Aunt's/Uncle's (maternal) residence	3	(4th from aunt/uncle-12th)
Aunt's/Uncle's (maternal) religion	8	(9th from aunt/uncle-12th)

Subject	House	Derivation
Aunt's/Uncle's (maternal) reputation/honor	9	(10th from aunt/uncle-12th)
Aunt's/Uncle's (maternal) resources	1	(2nd from aunt/uncle-12th)
Aunt's/Uncle's (maternal) secret enemies	11	(12th from aunt/uncle-12th)
Aunt's/Uncle's (maternal) spouse	6	(7th from aunt/uncle-12th)
Aunt's/Uncle's (maternal) surgery	7	(8th from aunt/uncle-12th)
Aunt's/Uncle's (maternal) terminal house	3	(4th from aunt/uncle-12th)
Aunt's/Uncle's (maternal) travel (distant or foreign)	8	(9th from aunt/uncle-12th)
Aunt's/Uncle's (maternal) travel (short distance)	2	(3rd from aunt/uncle-12th)
Aunt/Uncle (paternal)	6	(3rd from father-4th)
Aunt's/Uncle's (paternal) confinement	5	(12th from aunt/uncle-6th)
Aunt's/Uncle's (paternal) career	3	(10th from aunt/uncle-6th)
Aunt's/Uncle's (paternal) co-workers	11	(6th from aunt/uncle-6th)
Aunt's/Uncle's (paternal) death	1	(8th from aunt/uncle-6th)
Aunt's/Uncle's (paternal) employees	11	(6th from aunt/uncle-6th)
Aunt's/Uncle's (paternal) employer	3	(10th from aunt/uncle-6th)
Aunt's/Uncle's (paternal) father-in-law	3	(4th from aunt/uncle-spouse-12th)
Aunt's/Uncle's (paternal) friends	4	(11th from aunt/uncle-6th)
Aunt's/Uncle's (paternal) health/illness	11	(6th from aunt/uncle-6th)
Aunt's/Uncle's (paternal) hospitalization	5	(12th from aunt/uncle-6th)
Aunt's/Uncle's (paternal) inheritance	1	(8th from aunt/uncle-6th)
Aunt's/Uncle's (paternal) mother-in-law	9	(10th from aunt/uncle-spouse-12th)
Aunt's/Uncle's (paternal) neighbors	8	(3rd from aunt/uncle-6th)
Aunt's/Uncle's (paternal) open enemies	12	(7th from aunt/uncle-6th)
Aunt's/Uncle's (paternal) partner	12	(7th from aunt/uncle-6th)
Aunt's/Uncle's (paternal) physical condition	6	*
Aunt's/Uncle's (paternal) resources	7	(2nd from aunt/uncle-6th)
Aunt's/Uncle's (paternal) religion	2	(9th from aunt/uncle-6th)
Aunt's/Uncle's (paternal) reputation/honor	3	(10th from aunt/uncle-6th)
Aunt's/Uncle's (paternal) residence	9	(4th from aunt/uncle-6th)

Subject	House	Derivation
Aunt's/Uncle's (paternal) secret enemies	5	(12th from aunt/uncle-6th)
Aunt's/Uncle's (paternal) spouse	12	(7th from aunt/uncle-6th)
Aunt's/Uncle's (paternal) surgery	1	(8th from aunt/uncle-6th)
Aunt's/Uncle's (paternal) terminal house	9	(4th from aunt/uncle-6th)
Aunt's/Uncle's (paternal) travel (distant or foreign)	2	(9th from aunt/uncle-6th)
Aunt's/Uncle's (paternal) travel (short distance)	8	(3rd from aunt/uncle-6th)
Aura (human)	1	*
Authority Figures	10	*
Authority Symbols	10	*
Authority Figure's career	7	(10th from authority figure-10th)
Authority Figure's children	2	(5th from authority figure-10th)
Authority Figure's co-workers	3	(6th from authority figure-10th)
Authority Figure's confinement	9	(12th from authority figure-10th)
Authority Figure's death	5	(8th from authority figure-10th)
Authority Figure's employees	3	(6th from authority figure-10th)
Authority Figure's employer	7	(10th from authority figure-10th)
Authority Figure's father	1	(4th from authority figure-10th)
Authority Figure's father-in-law	7	(4th from authority figure-spouse-4th)
Authority Figure's friends	8	(11th from authority figure-10th)
Authority Figure's health/illness	3	(6th from authority figure-10th)
Authority Figure's hospitalization	9	(12th from authority figure-10th)
Authority Figure's inheritance	5	(8th from authority figure-10th)
Authority Figure's mother	7	(10th from authority figure-10th)

Subject	House	Derivation
Authority Figure's mother-in-law	1	(10th from authority figure-spouse-4th)
Authority Figure's neighbors	12	(3rd from authority figure-10th)
Authority Figure's open enemies	4	(7th from authority figure-10th)
Authority Figure's partner	4	(7th from authority figure-10th)
Authority Figure's physical condition	10	*
Authority Figure's religion	6	(9th from authority figure-10th)
Authority Figure's reputation/honor	7	(10th from authority figure-10th)
Authority Figure's residence	1	(4th from authority figure-10th)
Authority Figure's resources	11	(2nd from authority figure-10th)
Authority Figure's secret enemies	9	(12th from authority figure-10th)
Authority Figure's siblings	12	(3rd from authority figure-10th)
Authority Figure's spouse	4	(7th from authority figure-10th)
Authority Figure's surgery	5	(8th from authority figure-10th)
Authority Figure's terminal house	1	(4th from authority figure-10th)
Authority Figure's travel (distant or foreign)	6	(9th from authority figure-10th)
Authority Figure's travel (short distance)	12	(3rd from authority figure-10th)
Automobiles	3	*
Awards	10	*
B		
Bail	8	*
Bail Bonds	8	*
Bank Accounts	2	*
Bank Draft	2	*
Bankers	2	*
Bankruptcy	8	*

Subject	House	Derivation
Banks	2	*
Banquets	5	*
Baptism	9	*
Bar mitzvah	9	*
Barns	4	*
Barristers	*	See "Lawyers"
Bars	5	*
Bas mitzvah	9	*
Battles	7	*
Beauty Contests	*	See "Contests"
Bereavement	12	*
Bets	5	*
Bettors	5	*
Bicycles (used for pleasure)	5	*
Bicycles (used for transportation)	3	*
Bingo Games	5	*
Biofeedback	6	*
Birds (as pets)	6	*
Birds (wild)	12	*
Birth Certificate	3	*
Birth Control	8	*
Bishops	9	*
Blackmail	12	*
Boarders	6	*
Boarding Houses	4	*
Boats (house)	4	*
Boats (pleasure)	5	*
Bondage	12	*
Bonds (as investments)	5	*
Bookkeepers	6	*
Books	3	*
Boyfriend	5	*
Breast (artificial)	6	*
Bribery	8	*
Brothels	8	*
Brother	3	See "Siblings"
Brother-in-law	9	(3rd from spouse-7th, or 7th from sibling-3rd)
Brother-in-law's career	6	(10th from brother-in-law-9th)
Brother-in-law's children	1	(5th from brother-in-law-9th)
Brother-in-law's co-workers	2	(6th from brother-in-law-9th)

Subject	House	Derivation
Brother-in-law's confinement	8	(12th from brother-in-law-9th)
Brother-in-law's death	4	(8th from brother-in-law-9th)
Brother-in-law's employees	2	(6th from brother-in-law-9th)
Brother-in-law's employer	6	(10th from brother-in-law-9th)
Brother-in-law's father	12	(4th from brother-in-law-9th)
Brother-in-law's father-in-law	6	(4th from brother-in-law-spouse-3rd)
Brother-in-law's friends	7	(11th from brother-in-law-9th)
Brother-in-law's health/illness	2	(6th from brother-in-law-9th)
Brother-in-law's hospitalization	8	(12th from brother-in-law-9th
Brother-in-law's inheritance	4	(8th from brother-in-law-9th)
Brother-in-law's mother	6	(10th from brother-in-law-9th)
Brother-in-law's mother-in-law	12	(10th from brother-in-law-spouse-3rd)
Brother-in-law's neighbors	11	(3rd from brother-in-law-9th)
Brother-in-law's open enemies	3	(7th from brother-in-law-9th)
Brother-in-law's partner	3	(7th from brother-in-law-9th)
Brother-in-law's physical condition	9	*
Brother-in-law's religion	5	(9th from brother-in-law-9th)
Brother-in-law's reputation/honor	6	(10th from brother-in-law-9th)
Brother-in-law's residence	12	(4th from brother-in-law-9th)
Brother-in-law's resources	10	(2nd from brother-in-law-9th)
Brother-in-law's secret enemies	8	(12th from brother-in-law-9th)
Brother-in-law's siblings	11	(3rd from brother-in-law-9th)
Brother-in-law's spouse	3	(7th from brother-in-law-9th)
Brother-in-law's surgery	4	(8th from brother-in-law-9th)
Brother-in-law's terminal house	12	(4th from brother-in-law-9th)
Brother-in-law's travel (distant or foreign)	5	(9th from brother-in-law-9th)
Brother-in-law's travel (short distance)	11	(3rd from brother-in-law-9th)
Builders	4	*
Buildings	4	*
Burglars	12	*
Burglary	12	*

Subject	House	Derivation
Burials	4	*
Businesses	10	*
Business Associates	7	*
Business Locality	12	(3rd from business-10th)
Business Profits	11	(2nd from business-10th)
Busses	3	*
Buyer or Seller with whom Querent is dealing	7	*
C		
Cable Cars	3	*
Cablegrams	3	*
Cafeterias	6	*
Cameras	3	*
Campers	5	*
Captivity (place of)	12	*
Career (querent's)	10	*
Caretaker	6	*
Casinos	5	*
Cassettes (tapes or audio-visual)	3	*
Castration	8	*
Cattle	12	*
Caves	8	*
Cemeteries	4	*
Ceremony (religious)	9	*
Certificates	3	*
Cesspools	8	*
Chamber of Commerce	11	*
Chapels	9	*
Charge Accounts	8	*
Charitable Contributions	2	*
Charities	12	*
Charity Recipients	12	*
Check (drawn on a bank)	2	*
Checking Account	2	*
Child	5	*
Child (adopted)	5	*
Child (foster)	11	(5th from other-7th)
Child (illegitimate)	5	*
Child (querent's)	5	*
Child (step)	11	See "Stepchild"
Child (unborn)	5	*

Subject	House	Derivation
Child (unborn) (sex of)	5	*
Child's (adopted) career	2	(10th from adopted child-5th)
Child's (adopted) children	9	(5th from adopted child-5th)
Child's (adopted) co-workers	10	(6th from adopted child-5th)
Child's (adopted) confinement	4	(12th from adopted child-5th)
Child's (adopted) death	12	(8th from adopted child-5th)
Child's (adopted) employees	10	(6th from adopted child-5th)
Child's (adopted) employer	2	(10th from adopted child-5th)
Child's (adopted) father-in-law	2	(4th from adopted child-spouse-11th)
Child's (adopted) father	8	(4th from adopted child-5th)
Child's (adopted) friends	3	(11th from adopted child-5th)
Child's (adopted) health/illness	10	(6th from adopted child-5th)
Child's (adopted) hospitalization	4	(12th from adopted child-5th)
Child's (adopted) inheritance	12	(8th from adopted child-5th)
Child's (adopted) mother	2	(10th from adopted child-5th)
Child's (adopted) mother-in-law	8	(10th from adopted child-spouse-11th)
Child's (adopted) neighbors	7	(3rd from adopted child-5th)
Child's (adopted) open enemies	11	(7th from adopted child-5th)
Child's (adopted) partner	11	(7th from adopted child-5th)
Child's (adopted) physical condition	5	*
Child's (adopted) religion	1	(9th from adopted child-5th)
Child's (adopted) reputation/honor	2	(10th from adopted child-5th)
Child's (adopted) residence	8	(4th from adopted child-5th)
Child's (adopted) resources	6	(2nd from adopted child-5th)
Child's (adopted) secret enemies	4	(12th from adopted child-5th)
Child's (adopted) siblings	7	(3rd from adopted child-5th)
Child's (adopted) spouse	11	(7th from adopted child-5th)
Child's (adopted) surgery	12	(8th from adopted child-5th)
Child's (adopted) terminal house	8	(4th from adopted child-5th)
Child's (adopted) travel (distant or foreign)	1	(9th from adopted child-5th)
Child's (adopted) travel (short distance)	7	(3rd from adopted child-5th)

Subject	House	Derivation
Child's (foster) career	8	(10th from foster child-11th)
Child's (foster) children	3	(5th from foster child-11th)
Child's (foster) co-workers	4	(6th from foster child-11th)
Child's (foster) confinement	10	(12th from foster child-11th)
Child's (foster) death	6	(8th from foster child-11th)
Child's (foster) employees	4	(6th from foster child-11th)
Child's (foster) employer	8	(10th from foster child-11th)
Child's (foster) father	2	(4th from foster child-11th)
Child's (foster) father-in-law	8	(4th from foster child-spouse-5th)
Child's (foster) friends	9	(11th from foster child-11th)
Child's (foster) health/illness	4	(6th from foster child-11th)
Child's (foster) hospitalization	10	(12th from foster child-11th)
Child's (foster) inheritance	6	(8th from foster child-11th)
Child's (foster) mother	8	(10th from foster child-11th)
Child's (foster) mother-in-law	2	(10th from foster child-spouse-5th)
Child's (foster) neighbors	1	(3rd from foster child-11th)
Child's (foster) open enemies	5	(7th from foster child-11th)
Child's (foster) partner	5	(7th from foster child-11th)
Child's (foster) physical condition	11	*
Child's (foster) religion	7	(9th from foster child-11th)
Child's (foster) reputation/honor	8	(10th from foster child-11th)
Child's (foster) residence	2	(4th from foster child-11th)
Child's (foster) resources	12	(2nd from foster child-11th)
Child's (foster) secret enemies	10	(12th from foster child-11th)
Child's (foster) siblings	1	(3rd from foster child-11th)
Child's (foster) spouse	5	(7th from foster child-11th)
Child's (foster) surgery	6	(8th from foster child-11th)
Child's (foster) terminal house	2	(4th from foster child-11th)
Child's (foster) travel (distant or foreign)	7	(9th from foster child-11th)
Child's (foster) travel (short distance)	1	(3rd from foster child-11th)
Child's career	2	(10th from child-5th)
Child's co-workers	10	(6th from child-5th)
Child's confinement	4	(12th from child-5th)
Child's death	12	(8th from child-5th)
Child's employees	10	(6th from child-5th)
Child's employer	2	(10th from child-5th)
Child's father-in-law	2	(4th from child-spouse-11th)
Child's friends	3	(11th from child-5th)

Subject	House	Derivation
Child's health/illness	10	(6th from child-5th)
Child's higher education	1	(9th from child-5th)
Child's hospitalization	4	(12th from child-5th)
Child's inheritance	12	(8th from child-5th)
Child's mother-in-law	8	(10th from child-spouse-11th)
Child's neighbors	7	(3rd from child-5th)
Child's open enemies	11	(7th from child-5th)
Child's partner	11	(7th from child-5th)
Child's physical condition	5	*
Child's religion	1	(9th from child-5th)
Child's reputation/honor	2	(10th from child-5th)
Child's residence	8	(4th from child-5th)
Child's resources	6	(2nd from child-5th)
Child's secret enemies	4	(12th from child-5th)
Child's spouse	11	(7th from child-5th)
Child's surgery	12	(8th from child-5th)
Child's terminal house	8	(4th from child-5th)
Child's travel (distant or foreign)	1	(9th from child-5th)
Child's travel (short distance)	7	(3rd from child-5th)
Chiropodists	6	*
Chiropractors	6	*
Churches	9	*
Circus	5	*
City Hall	10	*
Civil Service	6	*
Civil Service Employees	6	*
Civil War	7	*
Clandestine Associates	12	*
Clandestine Matters	12	*
Clergy	9	*
Clergymen or Clergywomen	9	*
Clerks	6	*
Client	7	*
Clinics (medical)	12	*
Cloisters	12	*
Cloisters (convents)	12	*
Clothing	6	*
Club Members	11	*
Clubs	11	*
College Major (area of study)	9	*
Comets	9	*
Committee (for a fraternal group)	11	*

Subject	House	Derivation
Committee (for a political entity)	10	*
Commodities	6	*
Commodity Exchange	11	*
Communal Possessions	8	*
Commune	4	*
Commune's possessions	5	(2nd from commune-4th)
Communication	3	*
Communications Media	3	*
Community Property	8	*
Commuting	3	*
Competition	7	*
Compulsion	8	*
Computer Hardware	3	*
Computer Programmers	6	*
Computer Software	3	*
Concentration Camps	12	*
Conception	5	*
Confinement	12	*
Congress	11	*
Congress (members of)	11	*
Consulate	9	*
Contact Lenses	6	*
Contests	7	*
Contracts	3	*
Contractual Relationships	7	*
Conventions	11	*
Convents	12	*
Conversations	3	*
Convicts (escaped)	7	*
Copying Machines	3	*
Copyrights	3	*
Coronations	9	*
Coroner	8	*
Corporation	9	*
Corporation's profit or money	10	(2nd from corporation-9th)
Cosmetic Surgery	8	*
Cosmetics	5	*
Council Members	10	*
Counselor	7	*
Court Reporters	3	*
Court System	9	*
Courthouse	10	*

Subject	House	Derivation
Courtships	5	*
Cousin (maternal)	4	(5th from aunt/uncle-12th)
Cousin's (maternal) career	1	(10th from cousin-4th)
Cousin's (maternal) children	8	(5th from cousin-4th)
Cousin's (maternal) co-workers	9	(6th from cousin-4th)
Cousin's (maternal) confinement	3	(12th from cousin-4th)
Cousin's (maternal) death	11	(8th from cousin-4th)
Cousin's (maternal) employees	9	(6th from cousin-4th)
Cousin's (maternal) employer	1	(10th from cousin-4th)
Cousin's (maternal) father-in-law	1	(4th from cousin-spouse-10th)
Cousin's (maternal) friends	2	(11th from cousin-4th)
Cousin's (maternal) health/illness	9	(6th from cousin-4th)
Cousin's (maternal) hospitalization	3	(12th from cousin-4th)
Cousin's (maternal) inheritance	11	(8th from cousin-4th)
Cousin's (maternal) mother-in-law	7	(10th from cousin-spouse-10th)
Cousin's (maternal) neighbors	6	(3rd from cousin-4th)
Cousin's (maternal) open enemies	10	(7th from cousin-4th)
Cousin's (maternal) partner	10	(7th from cousin-4th)
Cousin's (maternal) physical condition	4	*
Cousin's (maternal) religion	12	(9th from cousin-4th)
Cousin's (maternal) reputation/honor	1	(10th from cousin-4th)
Cousin's (maternal) residence	7	(4th from cousin-4th)
Cousin's (maternal) resources	5	(2nd from cousin-4th)
Cousin's (maternal) secret enemies	3	(12th from cousin-4th)
Cousin's (maternal) siblings	6	(3rd from cousin-4th)
Cousin's (maternal) spouse	10	(7th from cousin-4th)
Cousin's (maternal) surgery	11	(8th from cousin-4th)
Cousin's (maternal) terminal house	7	(4th from cousin-4th)
Cousin's (maternal) travel (distant or foreign)	12	(9th from cousin-4th)
Cousin's (maternal) travel (short distance)	6	(3rd from cousin-4th)
Cousin (paternal)	10	(5th from aunt/uncle-6th)
Cousin's (paternal) career	7	(10th from cousin-10th)
Cousin's (paternal) children	2	(5th from cousin-10th)
Cousin's (paternal) co-workers	3	(6th from cousin-10th)
Cousin's (paternal) confinement	9	(12th from cousin-10th)
Cousin's (paternal) death	5	(8th from cousin-10th)

Subject	House	Derivation
Cousin's (paternal) employees	3	(6th from cousin-10th)
Cousin's (paternal) employer	7	(10th from cousin-10th)
Cousin's (paternal) father-in-law	7	(4th from cousin-spouse-4th)
Cousin's (paternal) friends	8	(11th from cousin-10th)
Cousin's (paternal) health/illness	3	(6th from cousin-10th)
Cousin's (paternal) hospitalization	9	(12th from cousin-10th) .
Cousin's (paternal) inheritance	5	(8th from cousin-10th)
Cousin's (paternal) mother-in-law	1	(10th from cousin-spouse-4th)
Cousin's (paternal) neighbors	12	(3rd from cousin-10th)
Cousin's (paternal) open enemies	4	(7th from cousin-10th)
Cousin's (paternal) partner	4	(7th from cousin-10th)
Cousin's (paternal) physical condition	10	*
Cousin's (paternal) religion	6	(9th from cousin-10th)
Cousin's (paternal) reputation/honor	7	(10th from cousin-10th)
Cousin's (paternal) residence	1	(4th from cousin-10th)
Cousin's (paternal) resources	11	(2nd from cousin-10th)
Cousin's (paternal) secret enemies	9	(12th from cousin-10th)
Cousin's (paternal) siblings	12	(3rd from cousin-10th)
Cousin's (paternal) spouse	4	(7th from cousin-10th)
Cousin's (paternal) surgery	5	(8th from cousin-10th)
Cousin's (paternal) terminal house	1	(4th from cousin-10th)
Cousin's (paternal) travel (distant or foreign)	6	(9th from cousin-10th)
Cousin's (paternal) travel (short distance)	12	(3rd from cousin-10th)
Co-workers	6	*
Co-worker's career	3	(10th from co-worker-6th)
Co-worker's children	10	(5th from co-worker-6th)
Co-worker's confinement	5	(12th from co-worker-6th)
Co-worker's death	1	(8th from co-worker-6th)
Co-worker's employees	11	(6th from co-worker-6th)
Co-worker's employer	3	(10th from co-worker-6th)
Co-worker's father	9	(4th from co-worker-6th)
Co-worker's father-in-law	3	(4th from co-worker-spouse-12th)
Co-worker's friends	4	(11th from co-worker-6th)
Co-worker's health/illness	11	(6th from co-worker-6th)
Co-worker's hospitalization	5	(12th from co-worker-6th)
Co-worker's inheritance	1	(8th from co-worker-6th)

Subject	House	Derivation
Co-worker's mother	3	(10th from co-worker-6th)
Co-worker's mother-in-law	9	(10th from co-worker-spouse-12th)
Co-worker's neighbors	8	(3rd from co-worker-6th)
Co-worker's open enemies	12	(7th from co-worker-6th)
Co-worker's partner	12	(7th from co-worker-6th)
Co-worker's physical condition	6	*
Co-worker's religion	2	(9th from co-worker-6th)
Co-worker's reputation/honor	3	(10th from co-worker-6th)
Co-worker's residence	9	(4th from co-worker-6th)
Co-worker's resources	7	(2nd from co-worker-6th)
Co-worker's secret enemies	5	(12th from co-worker-6th)
Co-worker's siblings	8	(3rd from co-worker-6th)
Co-worker's spouse	12	(7th from co-worker-6th)
Co-worker's surgery	1	(8th from co-worker-6th)
Co-worker's terminal house	9	(4th from co-worker-6th)
Co-worker's travel (distant or foreign)	2	(9th from co-worker-6th)
Co-worker's travel (short distance)	8	(3rd from co-worker-6th)
Crafts	6	*
Craft Associations or Organizations	6	*
Craftsmanship	6	*
Creation (querent's)	5	*
Credit	8	*
Credit Unions	8	*
Crematories	8	*
Criminal	7	*
Customer	7	*

D

Subject	House	Derivation
Dances	5	*
Dancing	5	*
Daughter-in-law	11	(7th from child-5th)
Daughter-in-law's career	8	(10th from child-spouse-11th)
Daughter-in-law's children	3	(5th from child-spouse-11th)
Daughter-in-law's co-workers	4	(6th from child-spouse-11th)
Daughter-in-law's confinement	10	(12th from child-spouse-11th)
Daughter-in-law's death	6	(8th from child-spouse-11th)
Daughter-in-law's employees	4	(6th from child-spouse-11th)
Daughter-in-law's employer	8	(10th from child-spouse-11th)
Daughter-in-law's father	2	(4th from child-spouse-11th)

Subject	House	Derivation
Daughter-in-law's friends	9	(11th from child-spouse-11th)
Daughter-in-law's health/illness	4	(6th from child-spouse-11th)
Daughter-in-law's hospitalization	10	(12th from child-spouse-11th)
Daughter-in-law's inheritance	6	(8th from child-spouse-11th)
Daughter-in-law's mother	8	(10th from child-spouse-11th)
Daughter-in-law's neighbors	1	(3rd from child-spouse-11th)
Daughter-in-law's open enemies	5	(7th from child-spouse-11th)
Daughter-in-law's partner	5	(7th from child-spouse-11th)
Daughter-in-law's physical condition	11	*
Daughter-in-law's religion	7	(9th from child-spouse-11th)
Daughter-in-law's reputation/honor	8	(10th from child-spouse-11th)
Daughter-in-law's residence	2	(4th from child-spouse-11th)
Daughter-in-law's resources	12	(2nd from child-spouse-11th)
Daughter-in-law's secret enemies	10	(12th from child-spouse-11th)
Daughter-in-law's siblings	1	(3rd from child-spouse-11th)
Daughter-in-law's surgery	6	(8th from child-spouse-11th)
Daughter-in-law's terminal house	2	(4th from child-spouse-11th)
Daughter-in-law's travel (distant or foreign)	7	(9th from child-spouse-11th)
Daughter-in-law's travel (short distance)	1	(3rd from child-spouse-11th)
Deacons	9	*
Death	8	*
Death Certificate	3	*
Deaths in the Family	11	(8th from family-4th)
Debtor	7	*
Debts	8	*
Delegates	7	*
Delegations	7	*
Delivery Person	3	*
Dentists	6	*
Detectives	8	*
Detention (places of)	12	*
Dictatorships	10	*
Disease	6	*
Distress	6	*
Divorce	7	*
Doctor (querent's)	7	*
Doctor's (querent's) Office/Clinic	12	(6th from doctor-7th)
Doctors	6	*

Subject	House	Derivation
Documents	3	*
Donations	8	*
Dowry	8	*
Dreams	8	*
Driver's license	3	*
Driver's license test	3	*
Drug Addiction	12	*
Drug Rehabilitation Center	12	*
Druggists	6	*
Druggists (querent's)	7	
Drugs (habit forming)	12	*
Drugs (illegal)	12	*
E		
Earning Capacity	2	*
Education (elementary or lower)	3	*
Education (higher)	9	*
Electric Company	10	*
Employees	6	*
Employee's children	10	(5th from employee-6th)
Employee's confinement	5	(12th from employee-6th)
Employee's death	1	(8th from employee-6th)
Employee's father	9	(4th from employee-6th)
Employee's father-in-law	3	(4th from employee-spouse-12th)
Employee's friends	4	(11th from employee-6th)
Employee's health/illness	11	(6th from employee-6th)
Employee's hospitalization	5	(12th from employee-6th)
Employee's inheritance	1	(8th from employee-6th)
Employee's mother	3	(10th from employee-6th)
Employee's mother-in-law	9	(10th from employee-spouse-12th)
Employee's neighbors	8	(3rd from employee-6th)
Employee's open enemies	12	(7th from employee-6th)
Employee's partner	12	(7th from employee-6th)
Employee's physical condition	6	*
Employee's religion	2	(9th from employee-6th)
Employee's reputation/honor	3	(10th from employee-6th)
Employee's residence	9	(4th from employee-6th)
Employee's resources	7	(2nd from employee-6th)
Employee's secret enemies	5	(12th from employee-6th)
Employee's siblings	8	(3rd from employee-6th)

Subject	House	Derivation
Employee's surgery	1	(8th from employee-6th)
Employee's terminal house	9	(4th from employee-6th)
Employee's travel (distant or foreign)	2	(9th from employee-6th)
Employee's travel (short distance)	8	(3rd from employee-6th)
Employees (civil service)	6	*
Employees (government)	6	*
Employer's	10	*
Employer's children	2	(5th from employer-10th)
Employer's confinement	9	(12th from employer-10th)
Employer's death	5	(8th from employer-10th)
Employer's father	1	(4th from employer-10th)
Employer's father-in-law	7	(4th from employer-spouse-4th)
Employer's friends	8	(11th from employer-10th)
Employer's health/illness	3	(6th from employer-10th)
Employer's hospitalization	9	(12th from employer-10th)
Employer's inheritance	5	(8th from employer-10th)
Employer's mother	7	(10th from employer-10th)
Employer's mother-in-law	1	(10th from employer-spouse-4th)
Employer's neighbors	12	(3rd from employer-10th)
Employer's open enemies	4	(7th from employer-10th)
Employer's partner	4	(7th from employer-10th)
Employer's physical condition	10	*
Employer's religion	6	(9th from employer-10th)
Employer's reputation/honor	7	(10th from employer-10th)
Employer's residence	1	(4th from employer-10th)
Employer's resources	11	(2nd from employer-10th)
Employer's secret enemies	9	(12th from employer-10th)
Employer's siblings	12	(3rd from employer-10th)
Employer's spouse	4	(7th from employer-10th)
Employer's surgery	5	(8th from employer-10th)
Employer's terminal house	1	(4th from employer-10th)
Employer's travel (distant or foreign)	6	(9th from employer-10th)
Employer's travel (short distance)	12	(3rd from employer-10th)
Employment (in authoritative position)	10	*
Employment (in nonautonomous position)	6	*
Encyclopedias	3	*

Subject	House	Derivation
End of the Matter	4	*
Enemy (open)	7	See "Open Enemy"
Enemy (secret)	12	See "Secret Enemy"
Entertainer	5	*
Entertainment	5	*
Entrenchments (earth fortifications)	4	*
Ephemerides	3	*
Escrows	8	*
Estates (inherited)	8	*
Estates (real property)	4	*
Etheric Body	1	*
Examinations (written or oral)	3	*
Executives	10	*
Exile	12	*
Explorers	9	*
Expressways	3	*
Extra-terrestrials	9	*
Eyeglasses	6	*
Eyes (artificial)	6	*
F		
False Teeth	6	*
Fame	10	*
Family	4	*
Family's resources	5	(2nd from family-4th)
Farm Products	4	*
Farmer	4	*
Farms	4	*
Father	4	*
Father's career	1	(10th from father-4th)
Father's co-workers	9	(6th from father-4th)
Father's confinement	3	(12th from father-4th)
Father's death	11	(8th from father-4th)
Father's employees	9	(6th from father-4th)
Father's employer	1	(10th from father-4th)
Father's friends	2	(11th from father-4th)
Father's health/illness	9	(6th from father-4th)
Father's hospitalization	3	(12th from father-4th)
Father's inheritance	11	(8th from father-4th)
Father's neighbors	6	(3rd from father-4th)
Father's open enemies	10	(7th from father-4th)
Father's partner	10	(7th from father-4th)

Subject	House	Derivation
Father's physical condition	4	*
Father's religion	12	(9th from father-4th)
Father's reputation/honor	1	(10th from father-4th)
Father's residence	7	(4th from father-4th)
Father's resources	5	(2nd from father-4th)
Father's secret enemies	3	(12th from father-4th)
Father's siblings	6	See "Aunts/Uncles"
Father's spouse	*	See "Mother" or "Stepmother"
Father's surgery	11	(8th from father-4th)
Father's terminal house	7	(4th from father-4th)
Father's travel (distant or foreign)	12	(9th from father-4th)
Father's travel (short distance)	6	(3rd from father-4th)
Father-in-law	10	(4th from spouse-7th)
Father-in-law's career	7	(10th from father-in-law-10th)
Father-in-law's co-workers	3	(6th from father-in-law-10th)
Father-in-law's confinement	9	(12th from father-in-law-10th)
Father-in-law's death	5	(8th from father-in-law-10th)
Father-in-law's employees	3	(6th from father-in-law-10th)
Father-in-law's employer	7	(10th from father-in-law-10th)
Father-in-law's friends	8	(11th from father-in-law-10th)
Father-in-law's health/illness	3	(6th from father-in-law-10th)
Father-in-law's hospitalization	9	(12th from father-in-law-10th)
Father-in-law's inheritance	5	(8th from father-in-law-10th)
Father-in-law's neighbors	12	(3rd from father-in-law-10th)
Father-in-law's open enemies	4	(7th from father-in-law-10th)
Father-in-law's partner	4	(7th from father-in-law-10th)
Father-in-law's physical condition	10	*
Father-in-law's religion	6	(9th from father-in-law-10th)
Father-in-law's reputation/honor	7	(10th from father-in-law-10th)
Father-in-law's residence	1	(4th from father-in-law-10th)
Father-in-law's resources	11	(2nd from father-in-law-10th)
Father-in-law's secret enemies	9	(12th from father-in-law-10th)
Father-in-law's siblings	12	(3rd from spouse-father-10th)
Father-in-law's surgery	5	(8th from father-in-law-10th)
Father-in-law's terminal house	1	(4th from father-in-law-10th)
Father-in-law's travel (distant or foreign)	6	(9th from father-in-law-10th)
Father-in-law's travel (short distance)	12	(3rd from father-in-law-10th)
Federal Bureau of Investigation (Govt. Agency)	10	*

Subject	House	Derivation
Federal Bureau of Investigation (investigations)	8	*
Fees	8	*
Feet (artificial)	6	*
Fertility	5	*
Festivals (nonreligious)	5	*
Festivals (religious)	9	*
Fetus	5	*
Fiance, Fiancee	7	*
Fields	4	*
Fines	8	*
Flea Markets	10	*
Flight Attendants	9	*
Food	6	*
Food Preparation	6	*
Food Service	6	*
Food Stamp Recipients	12	*
Food Stamps (used for purchasing power)	2	*
Foreign Countries	9	*
Foreigners	9	*
Foster Child	11	See "Child (foster)"
Franchises	10	*
Fraternal Groups/ Clubs/Organizations	11	*
Friends	11	*
Friend's career	8	(10th from friend-11th)
Friend's children	3	(5th from friends-11th)
Friend's co-workers	4	(6th from friend-11th)
Friend's confinement	10	(12th from friend-11th)
Friend's death	6	(8th from friend-11th)
Friend's employees	4	(6th from friend-11th)
Friend's employer	8	(10th from friend-11th)
Friend's father	2	(4th from friend-11th)
Friend's father-in-law	8	(4th from friend-spouse-5th)
Friend's friends	9	(11th from friend-11th)
Friend's health/illness	4	(6th from friend-11th)
Friend's hospitalization	10	(12th from friend-11th)
Friend's inheritance	6	(8th from friend-11th)
Friend's mother	8	(10th from friend-11th)
Friend's mother-in-law	2	(10th from friend-spouse-5th)
Friend's neighbors	1	(3rd from friend-11th)

Subject	House	Derivation
Friend's open enemies	5	(7th from friend-11th)
Friend's partner	5	(7th from friend-11th)
Friend's physical condition	11	*
Friend's religion	7	(9th from friend-11th)
Friend's reputation/honor	8	(10th from friend-11th)
Friend's residence	2	(4th from friend-11th)
Friend's resources	12	(2nd from friend-11th)
Friend's secret enemies	10	(12th from friend-11th)
Friend's siblings	1	(3rd from friend-11th)
Friend's spouse	5	(7th from friend-11th)
Friend's surgery	6	(8th from friend-11th)
Friend's terminal house	2	(4th from friend-11th)
Friend's travel (distant or foreign)	7	(9th from friend-11th)
Friend's travel (short distance)	1	(3rd from friend-11th)
Friends of the Family	2	(11th from family-4th)
Fugitive	7	*
Funeral Ceremony	9	*
Funeral Homes	4	*
Furniture	4	*
Future	2	*

G

Subject	House	Derivation
Gain (querent's)	2	*
Gambler	5	*
Gambling	5	*
Games	5	*
Garage Sales	4	*
Gardener	4	*
Gardens	4	*
Gas Company	10	*
Ghettos	12	*
Ghost Towns	12	*
Ghosts	12	*
Gifts (given to others)	2	*
Gifts (received from others)	8	*
Girlfriend	5	*
Goals	11	*
Godchild	11	(5th from other-7th)
Godchild's career	8	(10th from godchild-11th)
Godchild's children	3	(5th from godchild-11th)
Godchild's co-workers	4	(6th from godchild-11th)

Subject	House	Derivation
Godchild's confinement	10	(12th from godchild-11th)
Godchild's death	6	(8th from godchild-11th)
Godchild's employees	4	(6th from godchild-11th)
Godchild's employer	8	(10th from godchild-11th)
Godchild's father	2	(4th from godchild-11th)
Godchild's father-in-law	8	(4th from godchild-spouse-5th)
Godchild's friends	9	(11th from godchild-11th)
Godchild's health/illness	4	(6th from godchild-11th)
Godchild's hospitalization	10	(12th from godchild-11th)
Godchild's inheritance	6	(8th from godchild-11th)
Godchild's mother	8	(10th from godchild-11th)
Godchild's mother-in-law	2	(10th from godchild-spouse-5th)
Godchild's neighbors	1	(3rd from godchild-11th)
Godchild's open enemies	5	(7th from godchild-11th)
Godchild's partner	5	(7th from godchild-11th)
Godchild's physical condition	11	*
Godchild's religion	7	(9th from godchild-11th)
Godchild's reputation/honor	8	(10th from godchild-11th)
Godchild's residence	2	(4th from godchild-11th)
Godchild's resources	12	(2nd from godchild-11th)
Godchild's secret enemies	10	(12th from godchild-11th)
Godchild's siblings	1	(3rd from godchild-11th)
Godchild's spouse	5	(7th from godchild-11th)
Godchild's surgery	6	(8th from godchild-11th)
Godchild's terminal house	2	(4th from godchild-11th)
Godchild's travel (distant or foreign)	7	(9th from godchild-11th)
Godchild's travel (short distance)	1	(3rd from godchild-11th)
Gossip	3	*
Gossipers	3	*
Government	10	*
Government Agencies	10	*
Government Agencies (secret)	12	*
Government Employees	6	*
Government Programs	10	*
Governor	10	*
Grandchild	9	(5th from child-5th)
Grandchild's career	6	(10th from grandchild-9th)
Grandchild's children	1	(5th from grandchild-9th)

Subject	House	Derivation
Grandchild's co-workers	2	(6th from grandchild-9th)
Grandchild's confinement	8	(12th from grandchild-9th)
Grandchild's death	4	(8th from grandchild-9th)
Grandchild's employees	2	(6th from grandchild-9th)
Grandchild's employer	6	(10th from grandchild-9th)
Grandchild's father-in-law	6	(4th from grandchild-spouse-3rd)
Grandchild's friends	7	(11th from grandchild-9th)
Grandchild's health/illness	2	(6th from grandchild-9th)
Grandchild's hospitalization	8	(12th from grandchild-9th)
Grandchild's inheritance	4	(8th from grandchild-9th)
Grandchild's mother-in-law	12	(10th from grandchild-spouse-3rd)
Grandchild's neighbors	11	(3rd from grandchild-9th)
Grandchild's open enemies	3	(7th from grandchild-9th)
Grandchild's partner	3	(7th from grandchild-9th)
Grandchild's physical condition	9	*
Grandchild's religion	5	(9th from grandchild-9th)
Grandchild's reputation/honor	6	(10th from grandchild-9th)
Grandchild's residence	12	(4th from grandchild-9th)
Grandchild's resources	10	(2nd from grandchild-9th)
Grandchild's secret enemies	8	(12th from grandchild-9th)
Grandchild's siblings	11	(3rd from grandchild-9th)
Grandchild's spouse	3	(7th from grandchild-9th)
Grandchild's surgery	4	(8th from grandchild-9th)
Grandchild's terminal house	12	(4th from grandchild-9th)
Grandchild's travel (distant or foreign)	5	(9th from grandchild-9th)
Grandchild's travel (short distance)	11	(3rd from grandchild-9th)
Grandfather (maternal)	1	(4th from mother-10th)
Grandfather's (maternal) career	10	(10th from grandfather-1st)
Grandfather's (maternal) co-workers	6	(6th from grandfather-1st)
Grandfather's (maternal) confinement	12	(12th from grandfather-1st)
Grandfather's (maternal) death	8	(8th from grandfather-1st)
Grandfather's (maternal) employees	6	(6th from grandfather-1st)
Grandfather's (maternal) employer	10	(10th from grandfather-1st)
Grandfather's (maternal) friends	11	(11th from grandfather-1st)
Grandfather's (maternal) health/illness	6	(6th from grandfather-1st)

Subject	House	Derivation
Grandfather's (maternal) hospitalization	12	(12th from grandfather-1st)
Grandfather's (maternal) inheritance	8	(8th from grandfather-1st)
Grandfather's (maternal) neighbors	3	(3rd from grandfather-1st)
Grandfather's (maternal) open enemies	7	(7th from grandfather-1st)
Grandfather's (maternal) partner	7	(7th from grandfather-1st)
Grandfather's (maternal) physical condition	1	*
Grandfather's (maternal) resources	2	(2nd from grandfather-1st)
Grandfather's (maternal) religion	9	(9th from grandfather-1st)
Grandfather's (maternal) reputation/honor	10	(10th from grandfather-1st)
Grandfather's (maternal) residence	4	(4th from grandfather-1st)
Grandfather's (maternal) secret enemies	12	(12th from grandfather-1st)
Grandfather's (maternal) siblings	3	(3rd from grandfather-1st)
Grandfather's (maternal) surgery	8	(8th from grandfather-1st)
Grandfather's (maternal) terminal house	4	(4th from grandfather-1st)
Grandfather's (maternal) travel (distant or foreign)	9	(9th from grandfather-1st)
Grandfather's (maternal) travel (short distance)	3	(3rd from grandfather-1st)
Grandfather (paternal)	7	(4th from father-4th)
Grandfather's (paternal) career	4	(10th from grandfather-7th)
Grandfather's (paternal) co-workers	12	(6th from grandfather-7th)
Grandfather's (paternal) confinement	6	(12th from grandfather-7th)
Grandfather's (paternal) death	2	(8th from grandfather-7th)
Grandfather's (paternal) employees	12	(6th from grandfather-7th)
Grandfather's (paternal) employer	4	(10th from grandfather-7th)
Grandfather's (paternal) friends	5	(11th from grandfather-7th)
Grandfather's (paternal) health/illness	12	(6th from grandfather-7th)
Grandfather's (paternal) hospitalization	6	(12th from grandfather-7th)
Grandfather's (paternal) inheritance)	2	(8th from grandfather-7th)
Grandfather's (paternal) neighbors	9	(3rd from grandfather-7th)
Grandfather's (paternal) open enemies	1	(7th from grandfather-7th)
Grandfather's (paternal) partner	1	(7th from grandfather-7th)

Subject	House	Derivation
Grandfather's (paternal) physical condition	7	*
Grandfather's (paternal) resources	8	(2nd from grandfather-7th)
Grandfather's (paternal) religion	3	(9th from grandfather-7th)
Grandfather's (paternal) reputation/honor	4	(10th from grandfather-7th)
Grandfather's (paternal) residence	10	(4th from grandfather-7th)
Grandfather's (paternal) secret enemies	6	(12th from grandfather-7th)
Grandfather's (paternal) siblings	9	(3rd from grandfather-7th)
Grandfather's (paternal) surgery	2	(8th from grandfather-7th)
Grandfather's (paternal) terminal house	10	(4th from grandfather-7th)
Grandfather's (paternal) travel (distant or foreign)	3	(9th from grandfather-7th)
Grandfather's (paternal) travel (short distance)	9	(3rd from grandfather-7th)
Grandmother (maternal)	7	(10th from mother-10th)
Grandmother's (maternal) career	4	(10th from grandmother-7th)
Grandmother's (maternal) co-workers	12	(6th from grandmother-7th)
Grandmother's (maternal) confinement	6	(12th from grandmother-7th)
Grandmother's (maternal) death	2	(8th from grandmother-7th)
Grandmother's (maternal) employees	12	(6th from grandmother-7th)
Grandmother's (maternal) employer	4	(10th from grandmother-7th)
Grandmother's (maternal) friends	5	(11th from grandmother-7th)
Grandmother's (maternal) health/illness	12	(6th from grandmother-7th)
Grandmother's (maternal) hospitalization	6	(12th from grandmother-7th)
Grandmother's (maternal) inheritance	2	(8th from grandmother-7th)
Grandmother's (maternal) neighbors	9	(3rd from grandmother-7th)
Grandmother's (maternal) open enemies	1	(7th from grandmother-7th)
Grandmother's (maternal) partner	1	(7th from grandmother-7th)
Grandmother's (maternal) physical condition	7	*
Grandmother's (maternal) residence	10	(4th from grandmother-7th)
Grandmother's (maternal) religion	3	(9th from grandmother-7th)

Subject	House	Derivation
Grandmother's (maternal) reputation/honor	4	(10th from grandmother-7th)
Grandmother's (maternal) resources	8	(2nd from grandmother-7th)
Grandmother's (maternal) secret enemies	6	(12th from grandmother-7th)
Grandmother's (maternal) siblings	9	(3rd from grandmother-7th)
Grandmother's (maternal) surgery	2	(8th from grandmother-7th)
Grandmother's (maternal) terminal house	10	(4th from grandmother-7th)
Grandmother's (maternal) travel (distant or foreign)	3	(9th from grandmother-7th)
Grandmother's (maternal) travel (short distance)	9	(3rd from grandmother-7th)
Grandmother (paternal)	1	(10th from father-4th)
Grandmother's (paternal) career	10	(10th from grandmother-1st)
Grandmother's (paternal) co-workers	6	(6th from grandmother-1st)
Grandmother's (paternal) confinement	12	(12th from grandmother-1st)
Grandmother's (paternal) death	8	(8th from grandmother-1st)
Grandmother's (paternal) employees	6	(6th from grandmother-1st)
Grandmother's (paternal) employer	10	(10th from grandmother-1st)
Grandmother's (paternal) friends	11	(11th from grandmother-1st)
Grandmother's (paternal) health/illness	6	(6th from grandmother-1st)
Grandmother's (paternal) hospitalization	12	(12th from grandmother-1st)
Grandmother's (paternal) inheritance	8	(8th from grandmother-1st)
Grandmother's (paternal) neighbors	3	(3rd from grandmother-1st)
Grandmother's (paternal) open enemies	7	(7th from grandmother-1st)
Grandmother's (paternal) partner	7	(7th from grandmother-1st)
Grandmother's (paternal) physical condition	1	*
Grandmother's (paternal) resources	2	(2nd from grandmother-1st)
Grandmother's (paternal) religion	9	(9th from grandmother-1st)
Grandmother's (paternal) reputation/honor	10	(10th from grandmother-1st)
Grandmother's (paternal) residence	4	(4th from grandmother-1st)
Grandmother's (paternal) secret enemies	12	(12th from grandmother-1st)
Grandmother's (paternal) siblings	3	(3rd from grandmother-1st)
Grandmother's (paternal) surgery	8	(8th from grandmother-1st)

Subject	House	Derivation
Grandmother's (paternal) terminal house	4	(4th from grandmother-1st)
Grandmother's (paternal) travel (distant or foreign)	9	(9th from grandmother-1st)
Grandmother's (paternal) travel (short distance)	3	(3rd from grandmother-1st)
Grants	8	*
Gratuities	8	*
Graveclothes	4	*
Gravediggers	4	*
Graves	4	*
Gravestones	4	*
Great-grandchildren	1	(5th from grandchild-9th)
Groups	11	*
Guard	12	*
Guardian (child's)	2	(10th from child-5th)
Guardian (querent's)	10	*
Guru	9	*
Gymnasiums	5	*

H

Subject	House	Derivation
Hair Transplants	8	*
Hands (artificial)	6	*
Hardware (computer)	3	*
Heads of State	10	*
Healer	6	*
Healing	6	*
Healing (spiritual)	6	*
Healing Methods	6	*
Health-aiding Devices	6	*
Health/Illness (querent's)	6	*
Hearing Aids	6	*
Hidden Things	12	*
Hidden Treasures	4	*
Highways	3	*
Hobby	5	*
Home	4	*
Home under consideration (future)	7	*
Homesteads	4	*
Honeymoon	5	*
Honor	10	*

Subject	House	Derivation
Honor (querent's)	10	*
Hopes	11	*
Horses (domestic)	6	*
Horses (wild)	12	*
Hospitalization	12	*
Hospitals	12	*
Host/Hostess (airline)	9	*
Hotels	4	*
House of Commons	11	*
House of Representatives	11	*
Houseboats	4	*
Houses	4	*
Husband	7	See "Spouse"
Hymns	9	*
Hysterectomy	8	*
I		
Illness	6	See "Health/Illness"
Imprisonment	12	*
Inaugurations	9	*
Income	2	See "Resources"
Inferiors	6	*
Informer	12	*
Inheritance (genetic)	4	*
Inheritance (querent's)	8	*
Initiator of Action	1	*
In-law (father)	10	See "Father-in-law"
In-law (mother)	4	See "Mother-in-law"
In-laws (brother)	9	See "Brother-in-law"
In-laws (sister)	9	See "Sister-in-law"
Inquests	8	*
Insects	8	*
Installment Buying	8	*
Institutions	12	*
Insurance (as beneficiary)	8	*
Insurance (querent's)	8	*
Insurance (unemployment)	8	*
Insurance Adjusters	9	*
Insurance Company (as a corporation)	9	*
Insurance Proceeds	8	*

Subject	House	Derivation
Internal Revenue Service (Govt. Agency)	10	*
Internal Revenue Serice Tax Audit	8	*
Internment Camps	12	*
Inventions	5	*
Investments	5	*
J		
Jailers	12	*
Jails	12	*
Jewelry	5	*
Job	6	*
Joint Savings	8	*
Journeys	9	See "Travel"
Judges	10	*
Judicial System	9	*
Jury	11	*
K		
Kidnap	12	*
Kidnapper	12	*
Kindergarten	3	*
L		
Labor	6	*
Labor Unions	6	*
Laborer	6	*
Land	4	*
Landlord	10	*
Landlord (prospective)	7	*
Landscaping	4	*
Latrines	8	*
Law Enforcement	10	*
Lawns	4	*
Lawsuits	9	*
Lawyer (querent's)	7	*
Lawyers (in a court case)	9	*
Leaders	10	*
Leases	3	*
Leased Property	4	*
Legacy	8	*
Legal Adversaries	7	*

Subject	House	Derivation
Legislators	11	*
Legs (artificial)	6	*
Lending Agencies	8	*
Lessors (tenants)	6	*
Letters	3	*
Librarians	6	*
Library	3	*
Licenses	3	*
Loan Companies	8	*
Loans	8	*
Locality	3	*
Location	3	*
Lodgers	6	*
Lodges (fraternal)	11	*
Loss (querent's)	2	*
Lost Possessions	2	*
Lotteries	5	*
Love Affairs	5	*
Lover	5	*
M		
Magazines	3	*
Magistrates	10	*
Mail	3	*
Mail Box	3	*
Mail Order	3	*
Mailperson	3	*
Management	10	*
Manuscripts	3	*
Maps	3	*
Marine Corps	6	See "Armed Services"
Marriage	7	*
Marriage Certificate	3	*
Marriage Partner	7	See "Spouse"
Martial Arts	8	*
Matron of Jail	12	*
Mausoleums	4	*
Mayor	10	*
Mediation	7	*
Mediator	7	*
Medicaid	8	*
Medicare	8	*

Subject	House	Derivation
Medication	6	*
Medicine	6	*
Memorandums	3	*
Messages	3	*
Messenger	3	*
Metaphysics	9	*
Meteorite	9	*
Military Forces	6	*
Miner	4	*
Mines	4	*
Ministers	9	*
Miscarriages	5	*
Missing Persons	7	*
Mistresses	5	*
Monasteries	12	*
Money	2	See "Resources"
Money (from business)	11	(2nd from business-10th)
Money (lent to others)	2	*
Money (querent's)	2	*
Money (owed to others)	8	*
Money Market Funds	8	*
Monk	12	*
Mortgage Companies	8	*
Mortgages	8	*
Motels	4	*
Mother	10	*
Mother's career	7	(10th from mother-10th)
Mother's co-workers	3	(6th from mother-10th)
Mother's confinement	9	(12th from mother-10th)
Mother's death	5	(8th from mother-10th)
Mother's employees	3	(6th from mother-10th)
Mother's employer	7	(10th from mother-10th)
Mother's friends	8	(11th from mother-10th)
Mother's health/illness	3	(6th from mother-10th)
Mother's hospitalization	9	(12th from mother-10th)
Mother's inheritance	5	(8th from mother-10th)
Mother's neighbors	12	(3rd from mother-10th)
Mother's open enemies	4	(7th from mother-10th)
Mother's partner	4	(7th from mother-10th)
Mother's physical condition	10	*
Mother's religion	6	(9th from mother-10th)
Mother's reputation/honor	7	(10th from mother-10th)

Subject	House	Derivation
Mother's residence	1	(4th from mother-10th)
Mother's resources	11	(2nd from mother-10th)
Mother's secret enemies	9	(12th from mother-10th)
Mother's siblings	12	See "Aunts/Uncles"
Mother's spouse	*	See "Father" or "Stepfather"
Mother's surgery	5	(8th from mother-10th)
Mother's terminal house	1	(4th from mother-10th)
Mother's travel (distant or foreign)	6	(9th from mother-10th)
Mother's travel (short distance)	12	(3rd from mother-10th)
Mother-in-law	4	(10th from spouse-7th)
Mother-in-law's career	1	(10th from mother-in-law-4th)
Mother-in-law's co-workers	9	(6th from mother-in-law-4th)
Mother-in-law's confinement	3	(12th from mother-in-law-4th)
Mother-in-law's death	11	(8th from mother-in-law-4th)
Mother-in-law's employees	9	(6th from mother-in-law-4th)
Mother-in-law's employer	1	(10th from mother-in-law-4th)
Mother-in-law's friends	2	(11th from mother-in-law-4th)
Mother-in-law's health/illness	9	(6th from mother-in-law-4th)
Mother-in-law's hospitalization	3	(12th from mother-in-law-4th)
Mother-in-law's inheritance	11	(8th from mother-in-law-4th)
Mother-in-law's neighbors	6	(3rd from mother-in-law-4th)
Mother-in-law's open enemies	10	(7th from mother-in-law-4th)
Mother-in-law's partner	10	(7th from mother-in-law-4th)
Mother-in-law's physical condition	4	*
Mother-in-law's religion	12	(9th from mother-in-law-4th)
Mother-in-law's reputation/honor	1	(10th from mother-in-law-4th)
Mother-in-law's residence	7	(4th from mother-in-law-4th)
Mother-in-law's resources	5	(2nd from mother-in-law-4th)
Mother-in-law's secret enemies	3	(12th from mother-in-law-4th)
Mother-in-law's siblings	6	(3rd from spouse-mother-4th)
Mother-in-law's surgery	11	(8th from mother-in-law-4th)
Mother-in-law's terminal house	7	(4th from mother-in-law-4th)

Subject	House	Derivation
Mother-in-law's travel (distant or foreign)	12	(9th from mother-in-law-4th)
Mother-in-law's travel (short distance)	6	(3rd from mother-in-law-4th)
Motion Pictures	5	*
Motives (hidden, of accuser)	12	*
Movies	5	*
Murder	12	*
Music	5	*
N		
Narcotics	12	*
Navy	6	See "Armed Services"
Neighbors	3	*
Neighbor's career	12	(10th from neighbor-3rd)
Neighbor's children	7	(5th from neighbor-3rd)
Neighbor's co-workers	8	(6th from neighbor-3rd)
Neighbor's confinement	2	(12th from neighbor-3rd)
Neighbor's death	10	(8th from neighbor-3rd)
Neighbor's employees	8	(6th from neighbor-3rd)
Neighbor's employer	12	(10th from neighbor-3rd)
Neighbor's father	6	(4th from neighbor-3rd)
Neighbor's father-in-law	12	(4th from neighbor-spouse-9th)
Neighbor's friends	1	(11th from neighbor-3rd)
Neighbor's health/illness	8	(6th from neighbor-3rd)
Neighbor's hospitalization	2	(12th from neighbor-3rd)
Neighbor's inheritance	10	(8th from neighbor-3rd)
Neighbor's mother	12	(10th from neighbor-3rd)
Neighbor's mother-in-law	6	(10th from neighbor-spouse-9th)
Neighbor's open enemies	9	(7th from neighbor-3rd)
Neighbor's partner	9	(7th from neighbor-3rd)
Neighbor's physical condition	3	*
Neighbor's religion	11	(9th from neighbor-3rd)
Neighbor's reputation/honor	12	(10th from neighbor-3rd)
Neighbor's residence	6	(4th from neighbor-3rd)
Neighbor's resources	4	(2nd from neighbor-3rd)
Neighbor's secret enemies	2	(12th from neighbor-3rd)
Neighbor's siblings	5	(3nd from neighbor-3rd)
Neighbor's spouse	9	(7th from neighbor-3rd)
Neighbor's surgery	10	(8th from neighbor-3rd)

Subject	House	Derivation
Neighbor's terminal house	6	(4th from neighbor-3rd)
Neighbor's travel (distant or foreign)	11	(9th from neighbor-3rd)
Neighbor's travel (short distance)	5	(3nd from neighbor-3rd)
Neighborhood	3	*
Nephew (by marriage)	1	See "Brother/Sister-in-law's children"
Nephew (querent's)	7	See "Nieces/Nephews"
News	3	*
News Reports	3	*
Newspapers	3	*
Niece (by marriage)	1	See "Brother/Sister-in-law's children"
Niece (querent's)	7	See "Nieces/Nephews"
Niece's/Nephews	7	(5th from sibling-3rd)
Niece's/Nephew's career	4	(10th from niece/nephew-7th)
Niece's/Nephew's children	11	(5th from niece/nephew-7th)
Niece's/Nephew's co-workers	12	(6th from niece/nephew-7th)
Niece's/Nephew's confinement	6	(12th from niece/nephew-7th)
Niece's/Nephew's death	2	(8th from niece/nephew-7th)
Niece's/Nephew's employees	12	(6th from niece/nephew-7th)
Niece's/Nephew's employer	4	(10th from niece/nephew-7th)
Niece's/Nephew's father	10	(4th from niece/nephew-7th)
Niece's/Nephew's father-in-law	4	(4th from niece/nephew-spouse-1st)
Niece's/Nephew's friends	5	(11th from niece/nephew-7th
Niece's/Nephew's health/illness	12	(6th from niece/nephew-7th)
Niece's/Nephew's hospitalization	6	(12th from niece/nephew-7th)
Niece's/Nephew's inheritance	2	(8th from niece/nephew-7th)
Niece's/Nephew's mother	4	(10th from niece/nephew-7th)
Niece's/Nephew's mother-in-law	10	(10 from niece/nephew-spouse-1st)
Niece's/Nephew's neighbors	9	(3rd from niece/nephew-7th)
Niece's/Nephew's open enemies	1	(7th from niece/nephew-7th)
Niece's/Nephew's partner	1	(7th from niece/nephew-7th)
Niece's/Nephew's physical condition	7	*
Niece's/Nephew's religion	3	(9th from niece/nephew-7th)
Niece's/Nephew's reputation/honor	4	(10th from niece/nephew-7th)
Niece's/Nephew's residence	10	(4th from niece/nephew-7th)
Niece's/Nephew's resources	8	(2nd from niece/nephew-7th)

Subject	House	Derivation
Niece's/Nephew's secret enemies	6	(12th from niece/nephew-7th)
Niece's/Nephew's spouse	1	(7th from niece/nephew-7th)
Niece's/Nephew's surgery	2	(8th from niece/nephew-7th)
Niece's/Nephew's terminal house	10	(4th from niece/nephew-7th)
Niece's/Nephew's travel (distant or foreign)	3	(9th from niece/nephew-7th)
Niece's/Nephew's travel (short distance)	9	(3rd from niece/nephew-7th)
Notoriety	10	*
Nuclear Weapons	8	(2nd from war-7th)
Nuns	9	*
Nuns (cloistered)	12	*
Nursery School	3	*
Nurses	6	*
Nursing Homes	12	*

O

Subject	House	Derivation
Obsession	8	*
Occultism	8	*
Occupation	6	*
Office	6	*
Offspring	5	*
Oil	12	*
Oil Wells	12	*
Omens	8	*
One's Current Location	4	*
Open Enemy	7	*
Open Enemy's accomplice	12	(6th from open enemy-7th)
Open Enemy's career	4	(10th from open enemy-7th)
Open Enemy's children	11	(5th from open enemy-7th)
Open Enemy's confinement	6	(12th from open enemy-7th)
Open Enemy's death	2	(8th from open enemy-7th)
Open Enemy's employer	4	(10th from open enemy-7th)
Open Enemy's friends	5	(11th from open enemy-7th)
Open Enemy's health/illness	12	(6th from open enemy-7th)
Open Enemy's hospitalization	6	(12th from open enemy-7th)
Open Enemy's partner	1	(7th from open enemy-7th)
Open Enemy's physical condition	7	*
Open Enemy's religion	3	(9th from open enemy-7th)
Open Enemy's reputation/honor	4	(10th from open enemy-7th)
Open Enemy's residence	10	(4th from open enemy-7th)
Open Enemy's resources	8	(2nd from open enemy-7th)

Subject	House	Derivation
Open Enemy's siblings	9	(3rd from open enemy-7th)
Open Enemy's spouse	1	(7th from open enemy-7th)
Open Enemy's terminal house	10	(4th from open enemy-7th)
Ophthalmic Devices	6	*
Opponent	7	*
Orchards	4	*
Organ Donors	7	*
Organ Transplants	8	*
Organizations	11	*
Organized Charities	11	*
Organized Crime	8	*
Orphans	12	*
Orthodontic Devices	6	*
Orthopedic Devices	6	*
Other People (those not covered by another house)	7	*
Other Places	7	*
Others (over whom one has authority)	6	*
Outcome of Question	4	*

P

Subject	House	Derivation
Palimony	8	*
Pall Bearers	8	*
Parades	9	*
Parcel Post	3	*
Parent	*	See "Father" or "Mother"
Parents (as a unit)	4	*
Parent's resources	5	(2nd from parent-4th)
Parks	5	*
Parliament	10	*
Parties	5	*
Partner	7	*
Partner's career	4	(10th from partner-7th)
Partner's children	11	(5th from partner-7th)
Partner's co-workers	12	(6th from partner-7th)
Partner's confinement	6	(12th from partner-7th)
Partner's death	2	(8th from partner-7th)
Partner's employees	12	(6th from partner-7th)
Partner's employer	4	(10th from partner-7th)
Partner's father	10	(4th from partner-7th)
Partner's father-in-law	4	(4th from partner-spouse-1st)

Subject	House	Derivation
Partner's friends	5	(11th from partner-7th)
Partner's health/illness	12	(6th from partner-7th)
Partner's hospitalization	6	(12th from partner-7th)
Partner's inheritance	2	(8th from partner-7th)
Partner's mother	4	(10th from partner-7th)
Partner's mother-in-law	10	(10th from partner-spouse-1st)
Partner's neighbors	9	(3rd from partner-7th)
Partner's open enemies	1	(7th from partner-7th
Partner's partner	1	(7th from partner-7th)
Partner's physical condition	7	*
Partner's religion	3	(9th from partner-7th)
Partner's reputation/honor	4	(10th from partner-7th)
Partner's residence	10	(4th from partner-7th)
Partner's resources	8	(2nd from partner-7th)
Partner's secret enemies	6	(12th from partner-7th)
Partner's siblings	9	(3rd from partner-7th)
Partner's spouse	1	(7th from partner-7th)
Partner's surgery	2	(8th from partner-7th)
Partner's terminal house	10	(4th from partner-7th)
Partner's travel (distant or foreign)	3	(9th from partner-7th)
Partner's travel (short distance)	9	(3rd from partner-7th)
Partnerships	7	*
Patents	3	*
Patients	7	*
Peace Corps	6	*
Pension Funds	8	*
Periodicals	3	*
Persecutor	12	*
Personal Appearance	1	*
Personal Possessions	2	*
Perverts	12	*
Pets	6	*
Pet's confinement	5	(12th from pet-6th)
Pet's death	1	(8th from pet-6th)
Pet's health/illness	11	(6th from pet-6th)
Pet's physical condition	6	*
Pet's surgery	1	(8th from pet-6th)
Pet's terminal house	9	(4th from pet-6th)
Philanthropists	9	*
Philosophers	9	*
Philosophy	9	*

Subject	House	Derivation
Physical Body	1	*
Physical Examinations	6	*
Physician (querent's)	7	*
Physicians	6	*
Picnics	5	*
Pilots	9	*
Pilot's license	3	*
Pilot's license test	3	*
Place where business is carried on	6	*
Places (secluded or remote)	12	*
Plants	4	*
Plastic Surgery	8	*
Platonic Relationships	11	*
Playgrounds	5	*
Pleasures	5	*
Poisons	12	*
Police	10	*
Police Officers	10	*
Political Party (in power)	10	*
Political Party (out of power)	4	*
Politicians	10	*
Poolrooms	5	*
Pope	10	*
Possession by entities	12	*
Possessions (communal)	8	*
Possessions (joint)	8	*
Possessions (lost)	2	*
Possessions (movable)	2	*
Post Office	3	*
Postal Service	3	*
Poverty (querent's)	2	*
Power	10	*
Prayers	9	*
Preachers	9	*
Pregnancy	5	*
Preschool	3	*
Present	1	*
President	10	*
Press Corps	3	*
Priests	9	*
Prison Farms	12	*
Prisoner of War Camps	12	*

Subject	House	Derivation
Prisons	12	*
Produce	4	*
Produce Dealers	4	*
Produce Markets	4	*
Profession (querent's)	10	*
Professionals	10	*
Profit Sharing Plans	8	*
Profit (from business)	11	(2nd from business-10th)
Profit (from corporation)	10	(2nd from corporation-9th)
Profit (from publication)	10	(2nd from publication-9th)
Profit from travel	10	(2nd from travel-9th)
Programmer (computer)	6	*
Promotion (career)	10	*
Property (real)	4	*
Prosperity	2	*
Prosthetic Devices	6	*
Prostitutes	8	*
Psychiatrists	6	*
Psychic abilities	12	*
Psychosis	12	*
Public (the)	7	*
Public Funds	8	*
Public Status (querent's)	10	*
Publicity	10	*
Publisher	9	*
Publishing	9	*
Purchaser	7	*
Purchasing Agent	7	*

Q

Subject	House	Derivation
Quarrels	7	*
Querent	1	*
Querent's accidents	1	*
Querent's career	10	*
Querent's children	5	*
Querent's co-workers	6	*
Querent's confinement	12	*
Querent's employees	6	*
Querents employer	10	*
Querents father	4	*
Querent's father-in-law	10	(4th from spouse-7th)
Querent's friends	11	*

Subject	House	Derivation
Querent's health/illness	6	*
Querent's hospitalization	12	*
Querent's inheritance	8	*
Querent's length of life	1	*
Querent's mind	1	*
Querent's mother	10	*
Querent's mother-in-law	4	(10th from spouse-7th)
Querent's neighbors	3	*
Querent's open enemies	7	*
Querent's partner	7	*
Querent's physical condition	1	*
Querent's poverty	2	*
Querent's religion	9	*
Querent's reputation/honor	10	*
Querent's residence	4	*
Querent's resources	2	*
Querent's secret enemies	12	*
Querent's siblings	3	*
Querent's spouse	7	*
Querent's surgery	8	*
Querent's terminal house	4	*
Querent's thoughts	1	*
Querent's travel (distant or foreign)	9	*
Querent's travel (short distance)	3	*
R		
Rabbis	9	*
Racetracks	5	*
Radiation Therapy	11	(6th from physician-6th)
Radios	3	*
Raffles	5	*
Rail Transport	3	*
Railroad Yards	3	*
Railroads	3	*
Railway Stations	3	*
Rancher	4	*
Rank	10	*
Rapist	12	*
Real Estate	4	*
Real Estate (profit from)	5	(2nd from real estate-4th)
Recluse	12	*
Record Players	3	*

Subject	House	Derivation
Recreation	5	*
Recreational Vehicles	5	*
Red Cross	6	*
Reference Books	3	*
Reference Materials	3	*
Reform Schools	12	*
Reformatories	12	*
Refugee Camps	12	*
Relationship (contractual)	7	*
Relationships (romantic, with commitment)	7	*
Relationships (romantic, without commitment)	5	*
Religion	9	*
Religious Ceremony	9	*
Religious Sects	9	*
Remote Places	12	*
Renters (tenants)	6	*
Repairers	6	*
Report Cards	3	*
Reporter	3	*
Reports	3	*
Reports (from media)	3	*
Representatives	10	*
Reputation	10	*
Research	8	*
Residence	4	*
Residence (future, under consideration)	7	*
Resort Area	5	*
Resources (joint)	8	*
Resources (querent's)	2	*
Resources (property or real estate)	4	*
Rest Home	12	*
Restaurants (as a business)	10	*
Restaurants (as an eating place)	6	*
Retirement	12	*
Retirement Funds	8	*
Retirement Home	4	*
Retirement Income	2	*
Retirement Plans (financial)	8	*
Retreat (places of)	12	*

Subject	House	Derivation
Revolution	7	*
Ritual (religious)	9	*
Roads	3	*
Robber	7	*
Rodeos	5	*
Romance	5	*
Rooming Houses	4	*
Royalty	10	*
Rulers (of countries)	10	*
Rumors	3	*
Runaways	7	*
S		
Safe Deposit Box	2	*
Salary	2	*
Salespeople	3	*
Sanitarium	12	*
Satellites	9	*
Savings (joint)	8	*
Savings (querent's)	2	*
Scandal	10	*
Schools (higher education)	9	*
Schools (primary)	3	*
Schools (secondary)	5	*
Science	9	*
Secluded Places	12	*
Seclusion	12	*
Secret Enemy	12	*
Secret Enemy's accomplice	5	(6th from secret-enemy-12th)
Secret Enemy's career	9	(10th from secret-enemy-12th)
Secret Enemy's children	4	(5th from secret-enemy-12th)
Secret Enemy's confinement	11	(12th from secret-enemy-12th)
Secret Enemy's death	7	(8th from secret-enemy-12th)
Secret Enemy's employer	9	(10th from secret-enemy-12th)
Secret Enemy's friends	10	(11th from secret-enemy-12th)
Secret Enemy's health/illness	5	(6th from secret-enemy-12th)
Secret Enemy's hospitalization	11	(12th from secret-enemy-12th)
Secret Enemy's partner	6	(7th from secret-enemy-12th)
Secret Enemy's physical condition	12	*
Secret Enemy's religion	8	(9th from secret-enemy-12th)
Secret Enemy's reputation/honor	9	(10th from secret-enemy-12th)
Secret Enemy's residence	3	(4th from secret-enemy-12th)

Subject	House	Derivation
Secret Enemy's resources	1	(2nd from secret-enemy-12th)
Secret Enemy's siblings	2	(3rd from secret enemy-12th)
Secret Enemy's spouse	6	(7th from secret enemy-12th)
Secret Enemy's terminal house	3	(4th from secret-enemy-12th)
Secret Service	12	*
Secret Societies	12	*
Sects (religious)	9	*
Securities	2	*
Security Systems	4	*
Selectperson (town officer)	10	*
Self Destruction	12	*
Self Undoing	12	*
Seller or Buyer with whom Querent is dealing	7	*
Senate	11	*
Senators	10	*
Separation	7	*
Septic Tanks	8	*
Service	6	*
Settlements (agreements between people)	7	*
Settlements (financial)	8	*
Sewage Systems	8	*
Sewers	8	*
Sex (casual)	5	*
Sex (with commitment)	8	*
Sheriffs	10	*
Shopper	7	*
Show Business	5	*
Shrines	9	*
Shrubbery	4	*
Siblings	3	*
Siblings (adopted)	3	*
Sibling's career	12	(10th from sibling-3rd)
Sibling's children	7	See "Nieces/Nephews"
Sibling's co-workers	8	(6th from sibling-3rd)
Sibling's confinement	2	(12th from sibling-3rd)
Sibling's death	10	(8th from sibling-3rd)
Sibling's employees	8	(6th from sibling-3rd)
Sibling's employer	12	(10th from sibling-3rd)
Sibling's father-in-law	12	(4th from sibling-spouse-9th)
Sibling's friends	1	(11th from sibling-3rd)

Subject	House	Derivation
Sibling's health/illness	8	(6th from sibling-3rd)
Sibling's hospitalization	2	(12th from sibling-3rd)
Sibling's inheritance	10	(8th from sibling-3rd)
Sibling's mother-in-law	6	(10th from sibling-spouse-9th)
Sibling's neighbors	5	(3rd from sibling-3rd)
Sibling's open enemies	9	(7th from sibling-3rd)
Sibling's partner	9	(7th from sibling-3rd)
Sibling's physical condition	3	*
Sibling's religion	11	(9th from sibling-3rd)
Sibling's reputation/honor	12	(10th from sibling-3rd)
Sibling's residence	6	(4th from sibling-3rd)
Sibling's resources	4	(2nd from sibling-3rd)
Sibling's secret enemies	2	(12th from sibling-3rd)
Sibling's surgery	10	(8th from sibling-3rd)
Sibling's terminal house	6	(4th from sibling-3rd)
Sibling's travel (distant or foreign)	11	(9th from sibling-3rd)
Sibling's travel (short distance)	5	(3rd from sibling-3rd)
Sickness	6	*
Singing	5	*
Sister	3	See "Siblings"
Sister-in-law	9	(3rd from spouse-7th, or 7th from sibling-3rd)
Sister-in-law's career	6	(10th from sister-in-law-9th)
Sister-in-law's children	1	(5th from sister-in-law-9th)
Sister-in-law's confinement	8	(12th from Sister-in-law-9th)
Sister-in-law's co-workers	2	(6th from sister-in-law-9th)
Sister-in-law's death	4	(8th from sister-in-law-9th)
Sister-in-law's employees	2	(6th from sister-in-law-9th)
Sister-in-law's employer	6	(10th from sister-in-law-9th)
Sister-in-law's father	12	(4th from sister-in-law-9th)
Sister-in-law's father-in-law	6	(10th from sister-in-law-9th)
Sister-in-law's friends	7	(11th from sister-in-law-9th)
Sister-in-law's health/illness	2	(6th from sister-in-law-9th)
Sister-in-law's hospitalization	8	(12th from sister-in-law-9th
Sister-in-law's inheritance	4	(8th from sister-in-law-9th)
Sister-in-law's mother	6	(10th from sister-in-law-9th)
Sister-in-law's mother-in-law	12	(10th from sister-in-law-spouse-3rd)
Sister-in-law's neighbors	11	(3rd from sister-in-law-9th)
Sister-in-law's open enemies	3	(7th from sister-in-law-9th)
Sister-in-law's partner	3	(7th from sister-in-law-9th)

Subject	House	Derivation
Sister-in-law's physical condition	9	*
Sister-in-law's religion	5	(9th from sister-in-law-9th)
Sister-in-law's reputation/honor	6	(10th from sister-in-law-9th)
Sister-in-law's residence	12	(4th from sister-in-law-9th)
Sister-in-law's resources	10	(2nd from sister-in-law-9th)
Sister-in-law's secret enemies	8	(12th from sister-in-law-9th)
Sister-in-law's siblings	11	(3rd from sister-in-law-9th)
Sister-in-law's spouse	3	(7th from sister-in-law-9th)
Sister-in-law's surgery	4	(8th from sister-in-law-9th)
Sister-in-law's terminal house	12	(4th from sister-in-law-9th)
Sister-in-law's travel (distant or foreign)	5	(9th from sister-in-law-9th)
Sister-in-law's travel (short distance)	11	(3rd from sister-in-law-9th)
Slavery	12	*
Sleep	12	*
Social Security	8	*
Societies (fraternal)	11	*
Software (computer)	3	*
Son-in-law	11	(7th from child-5th)
Son-in-law's career	8	(10th from child-spouse-11th)
Son-in-law's children	3	(5th from child-spouse-11th)
Son-in-law's co-workers	4	(6th from child-spouse-11th)
Son-in-law's confinement	10	(12th from child-spouse-11th)
Son-in-law's death	6	(8th from child-spouse-11th)
Son-in-law's employees	4	(6th from child-spouse-11th)
Son-in-law's employer	8	(10th from child-spouse-11th)
Son-in-law's friends	9	(11th from child-spouse-11th)
Son-in-law's health/illness	4	(6th from child-spouse-11th)
Son-in-law's hospitalization	10	(12th from child-spouse-11th)
Son-in-law's inheritance	6	(8th from child-spouse-11th)
Son-in-law's mother	8	(10th from child-spouse-11th)
Son-in-law's neighbors	1	(3rd from child-spouse-11th)
Son-in-law's open enemies	5	(7th from child-spouse-11th)
Son-in-law's partner	5	(7th from child-spouse-11th)
Son-in-law's physical condition	11	*
Son-in-law's religion	7	(9th from child-spouse-11th)
Son-in-law's reputation/honor	8	(10th from child-spouse-11th)
Son-in-law's residence	2	(4th from child-spouse-11th)
Son-in-law's resources	12	(2nd from child-spouse-11th)
Son-in-law's secret enemies	10	(12th from child-spouse-11th)
Son-in-law's siblings	1	(3rd from child-spouse-11th)

Subject	House	Derivation
Son-in-law's surgery	6	(8th from child-spouse-11th)
Son-in-law's terminal house	2	(4th from child-spouse-11th)
Son-in-law's travel (distant or foreign)	7	(9th from child-spouse-11th)
Son-in-law's travel (short distance)	1	(3rd from child-spouse-11th)
Space Travel	9	*
Speculation	5	*
Speculators	5	*
Spies	12	*
Sponsors	7	*
Sporting Arenas	5	*
Sporting Events	5	*
Sports	5	*
Spouse	7	*
Spouse's Aunts/Uncles (maternal)	6	(3rd from spouse-mother-4th)
Spouse's Aunts/Uncles (paternal)	12	(3rd from spouse-father-10th)
Spouse's career	4	(10th from spouse-7th)
Spouse's co-workers	12	(6th from spouse-7th)
Spouse's confinement	6	(12th from spouse-7th)
Spouse's death	2	(8th from spouse-7th)
Spouse's employees	12	(6th from spouse-7th)
Spouse's employer	4	(10th from spouse-7th
Spouse's friends	5	(11th from spouse-7th
Spouse's health/illness	12	(6th from partner-7th)
Spouse's higher education	3	(9th from spouse-7th)
Spouse's hospitalization	6	(12th from spouse-7th
Spouse's inheritance	2	(8th from partner-7th)
Spouse's open enemies	1	(7th from spouse-7st)
Spouse's partner	1	(7th from spouse-7th)
Spouse's physical condition	7	*
Spouse's religion	3	(9th from spouse-7th)
Spouse's reputation/honor	4	(10th from spouse-7th)
Spouse's resources	8	(2nd from spouse-7th)
Spouse's secret enemies	6	(12th from spouse-7th)
Spouse's surgery	2	(8th from spouse-7th)
Spouse's terminal house	10	(4th from spouse-7th)
Spouse's travel (distant or foreign)	3	(9th from spouse-7th)
Spouse's travel (short distance)	9	(3rd from spouse-7th)
Stadiums	5	*
Status	10	*
Stepbrothers	*	See "Stepsiblings"

Subject	House	Derivation
Stepchild	11	(5th from spouse-7th)
Stepchild's career	8	(10th from stepchild-11th)
Stepchild's children	3	(5th from stepchild-11th)
Stepchild's co-workers	4	(6th from stepchild-11th)
Stepchild's confinement	10	(12th from stepchild-11th)
Stepchild's death	6	(8th from stepchild-11th)
Stepchild's employees	4	(6th from stepchild-11th)
Stepchild's employer	8	(10th from stepchild-11th)
Stepchild's father-in-law	8	(4th from stepchild-spouse-5th)
Stepchild's friends	9	(11th from stepchild-11th)
Stepchild's health/illness	4	(6th from stepchild-11th)
Stepchild's hospitalization	10	(12th from stepchild-11th)
Stepchild's inheritance	6	(8th from stepchild-11th)
Stepchild's mother	8	(10th from stepchild-11th)
Stepchild's mother-in-law	2	(10th from stepchild-spouse-5th)
Stepchild's neighbors	1	(3rd from stepchild-11th)
Stepchild's open enemies	5	(7th from stepchild-11th)
Stepchild's partner	5	(7th from stepchild-11th)
Stepchild's physical condition	11	*
Stepchild's religion	7	(9th from stepchild-11th)
Stepchild's reputation/honor	8	(10th from stepchild-11th)
Stepchild's residence	2	(4th from stepchild-11th)
Stepchild's resources	12	(2nd from stepchild-11th)
Stepchild's secret enemies	10	(12th from stepchild-11th)
Stepchild's siblings	1	(3rd from stepchild-11th)
Stepchild's spouse	5	(7th from stepchild-11th)
Stepchild's surgery	6	(8th from stepchild-11th)
Stepchild's terminal house	2	(4th from stepchild-11th)
Stepchild's travel (distant or foreign)	7	(9th from stepchild-11th)
Stepchild's travel (short distance)	1	(3rd from stepchild-11th)
Stepfather	4	(7th from mother-10th)
Stepfather's career	1	(10th from mother-spouse-4th)
Stepfather's co-workers	9	(6th from mother-spouse-4th)
Stepfather's confinement	3	(12th from mother-spouse-4th)
Stepfather's death	11	(8th from mother-spouse-4th)
Stepfather's employees	9	(6th from mother-spouse-4th)
Stepfather's employer	1	(10th from mother-spouse-4th)

Subject	House	Derivation
Stepfather's friends	2	(11th from mother-spouse-4th)
Stepfather's health/illness	9	(6th from mother-spouse-4th)
Stepfather's hospitalization	3	(12th from mother-spouse-4th)
Stepfather's inheritance	11	(8th from mother-spouse-4th)
Stepfather's neighbors	6	(3rd from mother-spouse-4th)
Stepfather's open enemies	10	(7th from mother-spouse-4th)
Stepfather's partner	10	(7th from mother-spouse-4th)
Stepfather's physical condition	4	*
Stepfather's religion	12	(9th from mother-spouse-4th)
Stepfather's reputation/honor	1	(10th from mother-spouse-4th)
Stepfather's residence	7	(4th from mother-spouse-4th)
Stepfather's resources	5	(2nd from mother-spouse-4th)
Stepfather's secret enemies	3	(12th from mother-spouse-4th)
Stepfather's siblings	6	(3rd from mother-spouse-4th)
Stepfather's surgery	11	(8th from mother-spouse-4th)
Stepfather's terminal house	7	(4th from mother-spouse-4th)
Stepfather's travel (distant or foreign)	12	(9th from mother-spouse-4th)
Stepfather's travel (short distance)	6	(3rd from mother-spouse-4th)
Stepmother	10	(7th from father-4th)
Stepmother's career	7	(10th from father-spouse-10th)
Stepmother's co-workers	3	(6th from father-spouse-10th)
Stepmother's confinement	9	(12th from father-spouse-10th)
Stepmother's death	5	(8th from father-spouse-10th)
Stepmother's employees	3	(6th from father-spouse-10th)
Stepmother's employer	7	(10th from father-spouse-10th)
Stepmother's friends	8	(11th from father-spouse-10th)
Stepmother's health/illness	3	(6th from father-spouse-10th)
Stepmother's hospitalization	9	(12th from father-spouse-10th)
Stepmother's inheritance	5	(8th from father-spouse-10th)
Stepmother's neighbors	12	(3rd from father-spouse-10th)
Stepmother's open enemies	4	(7th from father-spouse-10th)
Stepmother's partner	4	(7th from father-spouse-10th)
Stepmother's physical condition	10	*
Stepmother's religion	6	(9th from father-spouse-10th)
Stepmother's reputation/honor	7	(10th from father-spouse-10th)
Stepmother's residence	1	(4th from father-spouse-10th)
Stepmother's resources	11	(2nd from father-spouse-10th)

Subject	House	Derivation
Stepmother's secret enemies	9	(12th from father-spouse-10th)
Stepmother's siblings	12	(3rd from father-spouse-10th)
Stepmother's surgery	5	(8th from father-spouse-10th)
Stepmother's terminal house	1	(4th from father-spouse-10th)
Stepmother's travel (distant or foreign)	6	(9th from father-spouse-10th)
Stepmother's travel (short distance)	12	(3rd from father-spouse-10th)
Stepsibling (Father's stepchild)	2	(5th from father-spouse-10th)
Stepsibling (Mother's stepchild)	8	(5th from mother-spouse-4th)
Stepsibling's career	11	(10th from father-spouse-child-2nd)
Stepsibling's career	5	(10th from mother-spouse-child-8th)
Stepsibling's children	6	(5th from father-spouse-child-2nd)
Stepsibling's children	12	(5th from mother-spouse-child-8th)
Stepsibling's co-workers	7	(6th from father-spouse-child-2nd)
Stepsibling's co-workers	1	(6th from mother-spouse-child-8th)
Stepsibling's confinement	1	(12th from father-spouse-child-2nd)
Stepsibling's confinement	7	(12th from mother-spouse-child-8th)
Stepsibling's death	9	(8th from father-spouse-child-2nd)
Stepsibling's death	3	(8th from mother-spouse-child-8th)
Stepsibling's employees	7	(6th from father-spouse-child-2nd)
Stepsibling's employees	1	(6th from mother-spouse-child-8th)
Stepsibling's employer	11	(10th from father-spouse-child-2nd)
Stepsibling's employer	5	(10th from mother-spouse-child-8th)
Stepsibling's father	5	(4th from father-spouse-child-2nd)
Stepsibling's father-in-law	11	(4th from father-spouse-child-spouse-8th)

Subject	House	Derivation
Stepsibling's father-in-law	5	(4th from mother-spouse-child-spouse-2nd)
Stepsibling's friends	12	(11th from father-spouse-child-2nd)
Stepsibling's friends	6	(11th from mother-spouse-child-8th)
Stepsibling's health/illness	7	(6th from father-spouse-child-2nd)
Stepsibling's health/illness	1	(6th from mother-spouse-child-8th)
Stepsibling's hospitalization	1	(12th from father-spouse-child-2nd)
Stepsibling's hospitalization	7	(12th from mother-spouse-child-8th)
Stepsibling's inheritance	9	(8th from father-spouse-child-2nd)
Stepsibling's inheritance	3	(8th from mother-spouse-child-8th)
Stepsibling's mother	5	(10th from mother-spouse-child-8th)
Stepsibling's mother-in-law	5	(10th from father-spouse-child-spouse-8th)
Stepsibling's mother-in-law	11	(10th from mother-spouse-child-spouse-2nd)
Stepsibling's neighbors	4	(3rd from father-spouse-child-2nd)
Stepsibling's neighbors	10	(3rd from mother-spouse-child-8th)
Stepsibling's open enemies	8	(7th from father-spouse-child-2nd)
Stepsibling's open enemies	2	(7th from mother-spouse-child-8th)
Stepsibling's partner	8	(7th from father-spouse-child-2nd)
Stepsibling's partner	2	(7th from mother-spouse-child-8th)
Stepsibling's physical condition	2	(1st from father-spouse-child-2nd)
Stepsibling's physical condition	8	(1st from mother-spouse-child-8th)
Stepsibling's religion	10	(9th from father-spouse-child-2nd)

Subject	House	Derivation
Stepsibling's religion	4	(9th from mother-spouse-child-8th)
Stepsibling's reputation/honor	11	(10th from father-spouse-child-2nd)
Stepsibling's reputation/honor	5	(10th from mother-spouse-child-8th)
Stepsibling's residence	5	(4th from father-spouse-child-2nd)
Stepsibling's residence	11	(4th from mother-spouse-child-8th)
Stepsibling's resources	3	(2nd from father-spouse-child-2nd)
Stepsibling's resources	9	(2nd from mother-spouse-child-8th)
Stepsibling's secret enemies	1	(12th from father-spouse-child-2nd)
Stepsibling's secret enemies	7	(12th from mother-spouse-child-8th)
Stepsibling's siblings	4	(3rd from father-spouse-child-2nd)
Stepsibling's siblings	10	(3rd from mother-spouse-child-8th)
Stepsibling's spouse	8	(7th from father-spouse-child-2nd)
Stepsibling's spouse	2	(7th from mother-spouse-child-8th)
Stepsibling's surgery	9	(8th from father-spouse-child-2nd)
Stepsibling's surgery	3	(8th from mother-spouse-child-8th)
Stepsibling's terminal house	5	(4th from father-spouse-child-2nd)
Stepsibling's terminal house	11	(4th from mother-spouse-child-8th)
Stepsibling's travel (distant or foreign)	10	(9th from father-spouse-child-2nd)
Stepsibling's travel (distant or foreign)	4	(9th from mother-spouse-child-8th)
Stepsibling's travel (short distance)	4	(3rd from father-spouse-child-2nd)
Stepsibling's travel (short distance)	10	(3rd from mother-spouse-child-8th)

Subject	House	Derivation
Stepsisters	*	See "Stepsiblings"
Stereo Systems	3	*
Sterilization (sexual)	8	*
Steward/Stewardess (airline)	9	*
Stock Brokers	5	*
Stock Exchange	11	*
Stocks (as speculation)	5	*
Stolen Possessions	2	*
Strangers	7	*
Streetcars	3	*
Streets	3	*
Strikes (by labor unions)	6	*
Students	3	*
Subversion	12	*
Subways	3	*
Suicide	12	*
Superiors	10	*
Supervisors	10	*
Supreme Court	9	*
Surgeons	8	*
Surgery	8	*
Sweethearts	7	*
Synagogues	9	*
T		
Tape Recorders/Players	3	*
Taverns	5	*
Tax Assessors	8	*
Tax Audit	8	*
Tax Collector	8	*
Tax Consultants	8	*
Taxes	8	*
Taxi Cabs	3	*
Teachers	3	*
Telegrams	3	*
Telegraph System	3	*
Telephone Company	10	*
Telephones	3	*
Televisions	3	*
Temples	9	*
Tenants	6	*
Terminal House	4	*

Subject	House	Derivation
Terrorists	12	*
Tests (written or oral)	3	*
Textbooks	3	*
Theaters	5	*
Thief	7	*
Tips/Gratuities	8	*
Toilets	8	*
Tombs	4	*
Town Hall	10	*
Toys	3	*
Trade Unions	6	*
Trains	3	*
Transportation	3	*
Transportation Vehicles	3	*
Travel (long distance, duration, or foreign)	9	*
Travel (short distance or duration)	3	*
Travel (space)	9	*
Travel Agents	9	*
Travelers	9	*
Traveler's Checks	2	*
Treason	12	*
Treasure (buried or hidden)	4	*
Treasury Bonds	2	*
Treasury Notes	2	*
Trees	4	*
Trips	*	See "Travel"
Trust Funds	8	*
Tubal Ligation	8	*
Tutors	3	*
Twins	5	*
U		
US Postal Service	3	*
Unborn Child	5	*
Unborn Child's Sex	5	*
Uncle (maternal)	*	See "Aunts/Uncles (maternal)"
Uncle (paternal)	*	See "Aunts/Uncles (paternal)"
Undertaker	8	*

Subject	House	Derivation
Underworld	8	*
Unemployment Compensation	8	*
Utility Company	10	*
Utility Meters	11	*
V		
Vacations	5	*
Vasectomy	8	*
Vault	2	*
Vault (burial)	4	*
Vault (storage)	2	*
Vehicles of Transportation	3	*
Vehicles of War	9	(3rd from war-7th)
Verdict (in a court case)	4	*
Veterinarians	12	(6th from pet-6th)
Victim (murder)	8	*
Video Games	5	*
Video Players/Recorders	3	*
Video Tape Machines	3	*
Vineyards	4	*
Virginity	5	*
Visions	9	*
Visits	3	*
VISTA (Domestic Peace Corps)	6	*
Vitamins	6	*
Volunteer Service	6	*
W		
War	7	*
Warden of Jail	12	*
Wealth	2	*
Weapons of War	8	(2nd from War-7th)
Weather	4	*
Wedding	9	*
Welfare Recipients	12	*
Wells	4	*
Wicker Workers, Caners or Weavers	6	*
Widows	12	*
Wife	7	See "Spouse"
Wills	8	*
Wishes	11	*

Subject	House	Derivation
Witnesses (in a court case)	3	*
Women's liberation organizations	11	*
Workers	6	*
Workers Compensation	8	*
Working Environment	6	*
Writing	3	*
X		
Xerography	3	*
X-rays	11	(6th from physician-6th)
Y		
Yesterday	12	*
Z		
Zoo	6	*

PART V

LISTING BY HOUSES

FIRST HOUSE

Subject	Derivation
A	
Accidents to Querent	*
Aggressor (in war)	*
Alias	*
Astrologer (as querent)	*
Aunt's/Uncle's (maternal) resources	(2nd from aunt/uncle-12th)
Aunt's/Uncle's (paternal) death	(8th from aunt/uncle-6th)
Aunt's/Uncle's (paternal) inheritance	(8th from aunt/uncle-6th)
Aunt's/Uncle's (paternal) surgery	(8th from aunt/uncle-6th)
Aura	*
Authority Figure's father	(4th from authority figure-10th)
Authority Figure's mother-in-law	(10th from authority figure-spouse-4th)
Authority Figure's residence	(4th from authority figure-10th)
Authority Figure's terminal house	(4th from authority figure-10th)
B	
Brother-in-law's children	(5th from brother-in-law-9th)
C	
Child's (adopted) religion	(9th from adopted child-5th)
Child's (adopted) travel (distant or foreign)	(9th from adopted child-5th)
Child's (foster) neighbors	(3rd from foster child-11th)
Child's (foster) siblings	(3rd from foster child-11th)
Child's (foster) travel (short distance)	(3rd from foster child-11th)
Child's higher education	(9th from child-5th)
Child's religion	(9th from child-5th)
Child's travel (distant or foreign)	(9th from child-5th)
Cousin's (maternal) career	(10th from cousin-4th)
Cousin's (maternal) employer	(10th from cousin-4th)
Cousin's (maternal) father-in-law	(4th from cousin-spouse-10th)
Cousin's (maternal) reputation/honor	(10th from cousin-4th)
Cousin's (paternal) mother-in-law	(10th from cousin-spouse-4th)
Cousin's (paternal) residence	(4th from cousin-10th)
Cousin's (paternal) terminal house	(4th from cousin-10th)
Co-worker's death	(8th from co-worker-6th)

Subject	Derivation
Co-worker's inheritance	(8th from co-worker-6th)
Co-worker's surgery	(8th from co-worker-6th)
D	
Daughter-in-law's neighbors	(3rd from child-spouse-11th)
Daughter-in-law's siblings	(3rd from child-spouse-11th)
Daughter-in-law's travel (short distance)	(3rd from child-spouse-11th)
E	
Employee's death	(8th from employee-6th)
Employee's inheritance	(8th from employee-6th)
Employee's surgery	(8th from employee-6th)
Employer's father	(4th from employer-10th)
Employer's mother-in-law	(10th from employer-spouse-4th)
Employer's residence	(4th from employer-10th)
Employer's terminal house	(4th from employer-10th)
Etheric Body	*
F	
Father's career	(10th from father-4th)
Father's employer	(10th from father-4th)
Father's reputation/honor	(10th from father-4th)
Father-in-law's residence	(4th from father-in-law-10th)
Father-in-law's terminal house	(4th from father-in-law-10th)
Friend's neighbors	(3rd from friend-11th)
Friend's siblings	(3rd from friend-11th)
Friend's travel (short distance)	(3rd from friend-11th)
G	
Godchild's neighbors	(3rd from godchild-11th)
Godchild's siblings	(3rd from godchild-11th)
Godchild's travel (short distance)	(3rd from godchild-11th)
Grandchild's children	(9th from child-5th)
Grandfather (maternal)	(4th from mother-10th)
Grandfather's (maternal) physical condition	*
Grandfather's (paternal) open enemies	(7th from grandfather-7th)
Grandfather's (paternal) partner	(7th from grandfather-7th)
Grandmother (paternal)	(10th from father-4th)

Subject	Derivation
Grandmother's (maternal) open enemies	(7th from grandmother-7th)
Grandmother's (maternal) partner	(7th from grandmother-7th)
Grandmother's (paternal) physical condition	*
Great-grandchildren	(5th from grandchild-9th)
I	
Initiator of Action	*
M	
Mother's residence	(4th from mother-10th)
Mother's terminal house	(4th from mother-10th)
Mother-in-law's career	(10th from mother-in-law-4th)
Mother-in-law's employer	(10th from mother-in-law-4th)
Mother-in-law's reputation/honor	(10th from mother-in-law-4th)
N	
Neighbor's friends	(11th from neighbor-3rd)
Nephew (by marriage)	(5th from brother/sister-in-law-9th)
Niece (by marriage)	(5th from brother/sister-in-law-9th)
Niece's/Nephew's open enemies	(7th from niece/nephew-7th)
Niece's/Nephew's partner	(7th from niece/nephew-7th)
Niece's/Nephew's spouse	(7th from niece/nephew-7th)
O	
Open Enemy's partner	(7th from open enemy-7th)
Open Enemy's spouse	(7th from open enemy-7th)
P	
Partner's open enemies	(7th from partner-7th
Partner's partner	(7th from partner-7th)
Partner's spouse	(7th from partner-7th)
Personal Appearance	*
Pet's death	(8th from pet-6th)
Pet's surgery	(8th from pet-6th)
Physical Body	*
Present	*

Subject	Derivation
Q	
Querent	*
Querent's accidents	*
Querent's length of life	*
Querent's mind	*
Querent's physical condition	*
Querent's thoughts	*
S	
Secret Enemy's resources	(2nd from secret-enemy-12th)
Sibling's friends	(11th from sibling-3rd)
Sister-in-law's children	(5th from sister-in-law-9th)
Son-in-law's neighbors	(3rd from child-spouse-11th)
Son-in-law's siblings	(3rd from child-spouse-11th)
Son-in-law's travel (short distance)	(3rd from child-spouse-11th)
Spouse's open enemies	(7th from spouse-7st)
Spouse's partner	(7th from spouse-7th)
Stepchild's neighbors	(3rd from stepchild-11th)
Stepchild's siblings	(3rd from stepchild-11th)
Stepchild's travel (short distance)	(3rd from stepchild-11th)
Stepfather's career	(10th from mother-spouse-4th)
Stepfather's employer	(10th from mother-spouse-4th)
Stepfather's reputation/honor	(10th from mother-spouse-4th)
Stepmother's residence	(4th from father-spouse-10th)
Stepmother's terminal house	(4th from father-spouse-10th)
Stepsibling's co-workers	(6th from mother-spouse-child-8th)
Stepsibling's confinement	(12th from father-spouse-child-2nd)
Stepsibling's employees	(6th from mother-spouse-child-8th)
Stepsibling's health/illness	(6th from mother-spouse-child-8th)
Stepsibling's hospitalization	(12th from father-spouse-child-2nd)
Stepsibling's secret enemies	(12th from father-spouse-child-2nd)

SECOND HOUSE

Subject	Derivation
A	
Art (works of) (as a possession)	*
Aunt's/uncle's (maternal) neighbors	(3rd from aunt/uncle-12th)
Aunt's/uncle's (maternal) travel (short distance)	(3rd from aunt/uncle-12th)
Aunt's/uncle's (paternal) religion	(9th from aunt/uncle-6th)
Aunt's/uncle's (paternal) travel (distant or foreign)	(9th from aunt/uncle-6th)
Authority figure's children	(5th from authority figure-10th)
B	
Bank Accounts	*
Bank Draft	*
Bankers	*
Banks	*
Brother-in-law's co-workers	(6th from brother-in-law-9th)
Brother-in-law's employees	(6th from brother-in-law-9th)
Brother-in-law's health/illness	(6th from brother-in-law-9th)
C	
Charitable Contributions	*
Check (drawn on a bank)	*
Child's (adopted) career	(10th from adopted child-5th)
Child's (adopted) employer	(10th from adopted child-5th)
Child's (adopted) father-in-law	(4th from adopted child-spouse-11th)
Child's (adopted) mother	(10th from adopted child-5th)
Child's (adopted) reputation/honor	(10th from adopted child-5th)
Child's (foster) father	(4th from foster child-11th)
Child's (foster) mother-in-law	(10th from foster child-spouse-5th)
Child's (foster) residence	(4th from foster child-11th)
Child's (foster) terminal house	(4th from foster child-11th)
Child's career	(10th from child-5th)
Child's employer	(10th from child-5th)
Child's father-in-law	(4th from child-spouse-11th)
Child's reputation/honor	(10th from child-5th)
Cousin's (maternal) friends	(11th from cousin-4th)
Cousin's (paternal) children	(5th from cousin-10th)
Co-worker's religion	(9th from co-worker-6th)

Subject	Derivation
Co-worker's travel (distant or foreign)	(9th from co-worker-6th)
D	
Daughter-in-law's father	(4th from child-spouse-11th)
Daughter-in-law's residence	(4th from child-spouse-11th)
Daughter-in-law's terminal house	(4th from child-spouse-11th)
E	
Earning Capacity	*
Employee's religion	(9th from employee-6th)
Employee's travel (distant or foreign)	(9th from employee-6th)
Employer's children	(5th from employer-10th)
F	
Father's friends	(11th from father-4th)
Food Stamps (used for purchasing power)	*
Friend's father	(4th from friend-11th)
Friend's mother-in-law	(10th from friend-spouse-5th)
Friend's residence	(4th from friend-11th)
Friend's terminal house	(4th from friend-11th)
Friends of the family	(11th from family-4th)
Future	*
G	
Gain (querent's)	*
Gifts (given to others)	*
Godchild's father	(4th from godchild-11th)
Godchild's mother-in-law	(10th from godchild-spouse-5th)
Godchild's residence	(4th from godchild-11th)
Godchild's terminal house	(4th from godchild-11th)
Grandchild's co-workers	(6th from grandchild-9th)
Grandchild's employees	(6th from grandchild-9th)
Grandchild's health/illness	(6th from grandchild-9th)
Grandfather's (maternal) resources	(2nd from grandfather-1st)
Grandfather's (paternal) death	(8th from grandfather-7th)
Grandfather's (paternal) inheritance	(8th from grandfather-7th)
Grandfather's (paternal) surgery	(8th from grandfather-7th)
Grandmother's (maternal) death inheritance	(8th from grandmother-7th)
Grandmother's	(8th from grandmother-7th)

Subject	Derivation
Grandmother's (maternal) surgery	(8th from grandmother-7th)
Grandmother's (paternal) resources	(2nd from grandmother-1st)
Guardian (child's)	(10th from child-5th)
I	
Income	*
L	
Leases	*
Loss (querent's)	*
Lost Possessions	*
M	
Money	*
Money (lent to others)	*
Money (querent's)	*
Mother-in-law's friends	(11th from mother-in-law-4th)
N	
Neighbor's confinement	(12th from neighbor-3rd)
Neighbor's hospitalization	(12th from neighbor-3rd)
Neighbor's secret enemies	(12th from neighbor-3rd)
Niece's/Nephew's death	(8th from niece/nephew-7th)
Niece's/Nephew's inheritance	(8th from niece/nephew-7th)
Niece's/Nephew's surgery	(8th from niece/nephew-7th)
O	
Open enemies's death	(8 from open enemy-7th)
P	
Partner's death	(8th from partner-7th)
Partner's inheritance	(8th from partner-7th)
Partner's surgery	(8th from partner-7th)
Personal Possessions	*
Possessions (lost)	*
Possessions (movable)	*
Poverty (querent's)	*
Prosperity	*
Q	
Querent's poverty	*
Querent's resources	*

Subject	Derivation
R	
Resources (querent's)	*
Retirement Income	*
S	
Safe Deposit Box	*
Salary	*
Savings (querent's)	*
Secret Enemy's siblings	(3rd from secret enemy-12th)
Securities	*
Sibling's confinement	(12th from sibling3rd)
Sibling's hospitalization	(12th from sibling-3rd)
Sibling's secret enemies	(12th from sibling-3rd)
Sister-in-law's employees	(6th from sister-in-law-9th)
Sister-in-law's health/illness	(6th from sister-in-law-9th)
Sister-in-law's co-workers	(6th from sister-in-law-9th)
Son-in-law's residence	(4th from child-spouse-11th)
Son-in-law's terminal house	(4th from child-spouse-11th)
Spouse's death	(8th from spouse-7th)
Spouse's inheritance	(8th from partner-7th)
Spouse's surgery	(8th from spouse-7th)
Stepchild's mother-in-law	(10th from stepchild-spouse-5th)
Stepchild's residence	(4th from stepchild-11th)
Stepchild's terminal house	(4th from stepchild-11th)
Stepfather's friends	(11th from mother-spouse-4th)
Stepsibling (Father's stepchild)	(5th from father-spouse-10th)
Stepsibling's open enemies	(7th from mother-spouse-child-8th)
Stepsibling's partner	(7th from mother-spouse-child-8th)
Stepsibling's physical condition	(1st from father-spouse-child-2nd)
Stepsibling's spouse	(7th from mother-spouse-child-8th)
Stolen Possessions	*
T	
Traveler's Checks	*
Treasury Bonds	*
Treasury Notes	*
V	
Vault	*
Vault (storage)	*

Subject	Derivation
W Wealth	*

THIRD HOUSE

Subject	Derivation
A	
Adopted Brothers/Sisters	*
Advertising	*
Advertisers	*
Agents	*
Agreements (written)	*
Air Mail	*
Ambulances	*
Anonymous Letters	*
Atlas	*
Aunt's/Uncle's (maternal) mother-in-law	(10th from aunt/uncle-spouse-6th)
Aunt's/Uncle's (maternal) residence	(4th from aunt/uncle-12th)
Aunt's/Uncle's (maternal) terminal house	(4th from aunt/uncle-12th)
Aunt's/Uncle's (paternal) career	(10th from aunt/uncle-6th)
Aunt's/Uncle's (paternal) employer	(10th from aunt/uncle-6th)
Aunt's/Uncle's (paternal) father-in-law	(4th from aunt/uncle-spouse-12th)
Aunt's/Uncle's (paternal) reputation/honor	(10th from aunt/uncle-6th)
Authority Figure's co-workers	(6th from authority figure-10th)
Authority Figure's employees	(6th from authority figure-10th)
Authority Figure's health/illness	(6th from authority figure-10th)
Automobiles	*
B	
Bicycles (used for transportation)	*
Birth Certificate	*
Books	*
Brother	*
Brother-in-law's open enemies	(7th from brother-in-law-9th)
Brother-in-law's partner	(7th from brother-in-law-9th)
Brother-in-law's spouse	(7th from brother-in-law-9th)
Busses	*
C	
Cable Cars	*
Cablegrams	*

Subject	Derivation
Cameras	*
Cassettes (tapes or audio-visual)	*
Certificates	*
Child's (adopted) friends	(11th from adopted child-5th)
Child's (foster) children	(5th from foster child-11th)
Child's friends	(11th from child-5th)
Communication	*
Communications Media	*
Commuting	*
Computer Hardware	*
Computer Software	*
Contracts	*
Conversations	*
Copying Machines	*
Copyrights	*
Court Reporters	*
Cousin's (maternal) confinement	(12th from cousin-4th)
Cousin's (maternal) hospitalization	(12th from cousin-4th)
Cousin's (maternal) secret enemies	(12th from cousin-4th)
Cousin's (paternal) co-workers	(6th from cousin-10th)
Cousin's (paternal) employees	(6th from cousin-10th)
Cousin's (paternal) health/illness	(6th from cousin-10th)
Co-worker's career	(10th from co-worker-6th)
Co-worker's employer	(10th from co-worker-6th)
Co-worker's father-in-law	(4th from co-worker-spouse-12th)
Co-worker's mother	(10th from co-worker-6th)
Co-worker's reputation/honor	(10th from co-worker-6th)
Daughter-in-law's children	(5th from child-spouse-11th)

D

Subject	Derivation
Death Certificate	*
Delivery Person	*
Documents	*
Driver's license	*
Driver's license test	*

E

Subject	Derivation
Education (elementary or lower)	*
Employee's father-in-law	(4th from employee-spouse-12th)
Employee's mother	(10th from employee-6th)
Employee's reputation/honor	(10th from employee-6th)
Employer's health/illness	(6th from employer-10th)

Subject	Derivation
Encyclopedias	*
Ephemerides	*
Examinations (written or oral)	*
Expressways	*
F	
Father's confinement	(12th from father-4th)
Father's hospitalization	(12th from father-4th)
Father's secret enemies	(12th from father-4th)
Father-in-law's co-workers	(6th from father-in-law-10th)
Father-in-law's employees	(6th from father-in-law-10th)
Father-in-law's health/illness	(6th from father-in-law-10th)
Friend's children	(5th from friends-11th)
G	
Godchild's children	(5th from godchild-11th)
Gossip	*
Gossipers	*
Grandchild's open enemies	(7th from grandchild-9th)
Grandchild's partner	(7th from grandchild-9th)
Grandchild's spouse	(7th from grandchild-9th)
Grandfather's (maternal) neighbors	(3rd from grandfather-1st)
Grandfather's (maternal) siblings	(3rd from grandfather-1st)
Grandfather's (maternal) travel (short distance)	(3rd from grandfather-1st)
Grandfather's (paternal) religion	(9th from grandfather-7th)
Grandfather's (paternal) travel (distant or foreign)	(9th from grandfather-7th)
Grandmother's (maternal) religion	(9th from grandmother-7th)
Grandmother's (maternal) travel (distant or foreign)	(9th from grandmother-7th)
Grandmother's (paternal) neighbors	(3rd from grandmother-1st)
Grandmother's (paternal) siblings	(3rd from grandmother-1st)
Grandmother's (paternal) travel (short distance)	(3rd from grandmother-1st)
H	
Hardware (computer)	*
Highways	*
K	
Kindergarten	*

Subject	Derivation
L	
Leases	*
Letters	*
Library	*
Licenses	*
Locality	*
Location	*
M	
Magazines	*
Mail	*
Mail Box	*
Mail Order	*
Mailperson	*
Manuscripts	*
Maps	*
Marriage Certificate	*
Memorandums	*
Messages	*
Messenger	*
Mother's co-workers	(6th from mother-10th)
Mother's employees	(6th from mother-10th)
Mother's health/illness	(6th from mother-10th)
Mother-in-law's confinement	(12th from mother-in-law-4th)
Mother-in-law's hospitalization	(12th from mother-in-law-4th)
Mother-in-law's secret enemies	(12th from mother-in-law-4th)
N	
Neighbor's physical condition	*
Neighborhood	*
Neighbors	*
News	*
News Reports	*
Newspapers	*
Niece's/Nephew's religion	(9th from niece/nephew-7th)
Niece's/Nephew's travel (distant or foreign)	(9th from niece/nephew-7th)
Nursery School	*
O	
Open Enemy's religion	(9th from open enemy-7th)

Subject	Derivation
P	
Parcel Post	*
Partner's religion	(9th from partner-7th)
Partner's travel (distant or foreign)	(9th from partner-7th)
Patents	*
Periodicals	*
Pilot's license	*
Pilot's license test	*
Post Office	*
Postal Service	*
Preschool	*
Press Corps	*
Q	
Querent's neighbors	*
Querent's siblings	*
Querent's travel (short distance)	*
R	
Radios	*
Rail Transport	*
Railroad Yards	*
Railroads	*
Railway Stations	*
Record Players	*
Reference Books	*
Reference Materials	*
Report Cards	*
Reporter	*
Reports	*
Reports (from media)	*
Roads	*
Rumors	*
S	
Salespeople	*
Schools (primary)	*
Secret Enemy's residence	(4th from secret-enemy-12th)
Secret Enemy's terminal house	(4th from secret-enemy-12th)
Sibling's physical condition	*
Siblings	*
Siblings (adopted)	*

Subject	Derivation
Sister	*
Sister-in-law's open enemies	(7th from sister-in-law-9th)
Sister-in-law's partner	(7th from sister-in-law-9th)
Sister-in-law's spouse	(7th from sister-in-law-9th)
Software (computer)	*
Son-in-law's children	(5th from child-spouse-11th)
Spouse's higher education	(9th from spouse-7th)
Spouse's religion	(9th from spouse-7th)
Spouse's travel (distant or foreign)	(9th from spouse-7th)
Stepfather's confinement	(12th from mother-spouse-4th)
Stepfather's hospitalization	(12th from mother-spouse-4th)
Stepfather's secret enemies	(12th from mother-spouse-4th)
Stepmother's co-workers	(6th from father-spouse-10th)
Stepmother's employees	(6th from father-spouse-10th)
Stepmother's health/illness	(6th from father-spouse-10th)
Stepsibling's death	(8th from mother-spouse-child-8th)
Stepsibling's inheritance	(8th from mother-spouse-child-8th)
Stepsibling's resources	(2nd from father-spouse-child-2nd)
Stepsibling's surgery	(8th from mother-spouse-child-8th)
Stereo Systems	*
Streetcars	*
Streets	*
Students	*
Subways	*
T	
Tape Recorders/Players	*
Taxi Cabs	*
Teachers	*
Telegrams	*
Telegraph System	*
Telephones	*
Televisions	*
Tests (written or oral)	*
Textbooks	*
Toys	*
Trains	*
Transportation	*
Transportation Vehicles	*
Travel (short distance or duration)	*
Tutors	*

Subject	Derivation
U	
US Postal Service	*
V	
Vehicles of Transportation	*
Video Players/Recorders	*
Video Tape Machines	*
Visits	*
W	
Witnesses (in a court case)	*
Writing	*
X	
Xerography	*

FOURTH HOUSE

Subject	Derivation
A	
Agriculture	*
Ancestors	*
Antiques	*
Artifacts	*
Aunt'a/Uncle's (paternal) friends	(11th from aunt/uncle-6th)
Authority Figure's open enemies	(7th from authority figure-10th)
Authority Figure's partner	(7th from authority figure-10th)
Authority Figure's spouse	(7th from authority figure-10th)
B	
Barns	*
Boarding Houses	*
Boats (house)	*
Brother-in-law's death	(8th from brother-in-law-9th)
Brother-in-law's inheritance	(8th from brother-in-law-9th)
Brother-in-law's surgery	(8th from brother-in-law-9th)
Builders	*
Buildings	*
Burials	*
C	
Cemeteries	*
Child's (adopted) confinement	(12th from adopted child-5th)
Child's (adopted) hospitalization	(12th from adopted child-5th)
Child's (adopted) secret enemies	(12th from adopted child-5th)
Child's (foster) co-workers	(6th from foster child-11th)
Child's (foster) employees	(6th from foster child-11th)
Child's (foster) health/illness	(6th from foster child-11th)
Child's confinement	(12th from child-5th)
Child's hospitalization	(12th from child-5th)
Child's secret enemies	(12th from child-5th)
Commune	*
Cousin (maternal)	(5th from aunt/uncle-12th)
Cousin's (maternal) physical condition	*
Cousin's (paternal) open enemies	(7th from cousin-10th)
Cousin's (paternal) partner	(7th from cousin-10th)
Cousin's (paternal) spouse	(7th from cousin-10th)

Subject	Derivation
Co-worker's friends	(11th from co-worker-6th)
D	
Daughter-in-law's co-workers	(6th from child-spouse-11th)
Daughter-in-law's employees	(6th from child-spouse-11th)
Daughter-in-law's health/illness	(6th from child-spouse-11th)
E	
Employee's friends	(11th from employee-6th)
Employer's open enemies	(7th from employer-10th)
Employer's partner	(7th from employer-10th)
Employer's spouse	(7th from employer-10th)
End of the matter	*
Entrenchments (earth fortifications)	*
Estates (real property)	*
F	
Family	*
Farm Products	*
Farmer	*
Farms	*
Father	*
Father's physical condition	*
Father-in-law's open enemies	(7th from father-in-law-10th)
Father-in-law's partner	(7th from father-in-law-10th)
Fields	*
Friend's co-workers	(6th from friend-11th)
Friend's employees	(6th from friend-11th)
Friend's health/illness	(6th from friend-11th)
Funeral Homes	*
Furniture	*
G	
Garage Sales	*
Gardener	*
Gardens	*
Godchild's co-workers	(6th from godchild-11th)
Godchild's employees	(6th from godchild-11th)
Godchild's health/illness	(6th from godchild-11th)
Grandchild's death	(8th from grandchild-9th)
Grandchild's inheritance	(8th from grandchild-9th)
Grandchild's surgery	(8th from grandchild-9th)

Subject	Derivation
Grandfather's (maternal) residence	(4th from grandfather-1st)
Grandfather's (maternal) terminal house	(4th from grandfather-1st)
Grandfather's (paternal) career	(10th from grandfather-7th)
Grandfather's (paternal) employer	(10th from grandfather-7th)
Grandfather's (paternal) reputation/honor	(10th from grandfather-7th)
Grandmother's (maternal) career	(10th from grandmother-7th)
Grandmother's (maternal) employer	(10th from grandmother-7th)
Grandmother's (maternal) reputation/honor	(10th from grandmother-7th)
Grandmother's (paternal) residence	(4th from grandmother-1st)
Grandmother's (paternal) terminal house	(4th from grandmother-1st)
Graveclothes	*
Gravediggers	*
Graves	*
Gravestones	*
H	
Hidden Treasures	*
Home	*
Homesteads	*
Hotels	*
Houseboats	*
Houses	*
I	
Inheritance (genetic)	*
In-law (mother)	(10th from spouse-7th)
L	
Land	*
Landscaping	*
Lawns	*
Leased Property	*
Location	*
M	
Mausoleums	*
Miner	*
Mines	*

Subject	Derivation
Motels	*
Mother's open enemies	(7th from mother-10th)
Mother's partner	(7th from mother-10th)
Mother-in-law	(10th from spouse-7th)
Mother-in-law's physical condition	*
N	
Neighbor's resources	(2nd from neighbor-3rd)
Niece's/Nephew's career	(10th from niece/nephew-7th)
Niece's/Nephew's employer	(10th from niece/nephew-7th)
Niece's/Nephew's father-in-law	(4th from niece/nephew-spouse-1st)
Niece's/Nephew's mother	(10th from niece/nephew-7th)
Niece's/Nephew's reputation/honor	(10th from niece/nephew-7th)
O	
One's current location	*
Open Enemy's career	(10th from open enemy-7th)
Open Enemy's employer	(10th from open enemy-7th)
Open Enemy's reputation/honor	(10th from open enemy-7th)
Orchards	*
Outcome of Question	*
P	
Parents (as a unit)	*
Partner's career	(10th from partner-7th)
Partner's employer	(10th from partner-7th)
Partner's father-in-law	(4th from partner-spouse-1st)
Partner's mother	(10th from partner-7th)
Partner's reputation/honor	(10th from partner-7th)
Plants	*
Political Party (out of power)	*
Produce	*
Produce Dealers	*
Produce Markets	*
Property (real)	*
Q	
Querent's father	*
Querent's mother-in-law	(10th from spouse-7th)
Querent's residence	(10th from spouse-7th)
Querent's terminal house	(10th from spouse-7th

Subject	Derivation
R	
Rancher	*
Real Estate	*
Residence	*
Resources, (property or real estate)	*
Retirement Home	*
Rooming Houses	*
S	
Secret Enemy's children	(5th from secret-enemy-12th)
Security Systems	*
Shrubbery	*
Sibling's resources	(2nd from sibling-3rd)
Sister-in-law's death	(8th from sister-in-law-9th)
Sister-in-law's inheritance	(8th from sister-in-law-9th)
Sister-in-law's surgery	(8th from sister-in-law-9th)
Son-in-law's co-workers	(6th from child-spouse-11th)
Son-in-law's employees	(6th from child-spouse-11th)
Son-in-law's health/illness	(6th from child-spouse-11th)
Spouse's career	(10th from spouse-7th)
Spouse's employer	(10th from spouse-7th
Spouse's reputation/honor	(10th from spouse-7th)
Stepchild's co-workers	(6th from stepchild-11th)
Stepchild's employees	(6th from stepchild-11th
Stepchild's health/illness	(6th from stepchild-11th)
Stepfather	(7th from mother-10th)
Stepfather's physical condition	*
Stepmother's open enemies	(7th from father-spouse-10th)
Stepmother's partner	(7th from father-spouse-10th)
Stepsibling's neighbors	(3rd from father-spouse-child-2nd)
Stepsibling's religion	(9th from mother-spouse-child-8th)
Stepsibling's siblings	(3rd from father-spouse-child-2nd)
Stepsibling's travel (distant or foreign)	(9th from mother-spouse-child-8th)
Stepsibling's travel (short distance)	(3rd from father-spouse-child-2nd)
T	
Terminal House	*
Tombs	*
Treasure (buried or hidden)	*
Trees	*

Subject	Derivation
V	
Vault (burial)	*
Verdict (in a court case)	*
Vineyards	*
W	
Weather	*
Wells	*

FIFTH HOUSE

Subject	Derivation
A	
Abortion (spontaneous)	*
Acting	*
Adopted Child	*
Adultery	*
Adventures	*
Ambassadors (from other countries)	*
Amusement Areas	*
Amusements	*
Arcade Games	*
Arenas	*
Art (works of) (as an investment)	*
Artificial Insemination	*
Aunt's/Uncle's (maternal) co-workers	(6th from aunt/uncle-12th)
Aunt's/Uncle's (maternal) employees	(6th from aunt/uncle-12th)
Aunt's/Uncle's (maternal) health/illness	(6th from aunt/uncle-12th)
Aunt's/Uncle's (paternal) confinement	(12th from aunt/uncle-6th)
Aunt's/Uncle's (paternal) hospitalization	(12th from aunt/uncle-6th)
Aunt's/Uncle's (paternal) secret enemies	(12th from aunt/uncle-6th)
Authority Figure's death	(8th from authority figure-10th)
Authority Figure's inheritance	(8th from authority figure-10th)
Authority Figure's surgery	(8th from authority figure-10th)
B	
Banquets	*
Bars	*
Bets	*
Bettors	*
Bicycles (used for pleasure)	*
Bingo Games	*
Boats (pleasure)	*
Bonds (as investments)	*
Boyfriend	*
Brother-in-law's religion	(9th from brother-in-law-9th)

Subject	Derivation
Brother-in-law's travel (distant or foreign)	(9th from brother-in-law-9th)
C	
Campers	*
Casinos	*
Child	*
Child (adopted)	*
Child (illegitimate)	*
Child (querent's)	*
Child (unborn)	*
Child (unborn) (sex of)	*
Child's (adopted) physical condition	*
Child's (foster) open enemies	(7th from foster child-11th)
Child's (foster) partner	(7th from foster child-11th)
Child's (foster) spouse	(7th from foster child-11th)
Child's physical condition	*
Circus	*
Communes (possessions)	(2nd from commune-4th)
Conception	*
Cosmetics	*
Courtships	*
Cousin's (maternal) resources	(2nd from cousin-4th)
Cousin's (paternal) death	(8th from cousin-10th)
Cousin's (paternal) inheritance	(8th from cousin-10th)
Cousin's (paternal) surgery	(8th from cousin-10th)
Co-worker's confinement	(12th from co-worker-6th)
Co-worker's hospitalization	(12th from co-worker-6th)
Co-worker's secret enemies	(12th from co-worker-6th)
Creation (querent's)	*
D	
Dances	*
Dancing	*
Daughter-in-law's open enemies	(7th from child-spouse-11th)
Daughter-in-law's partner	(7th from child-spouse-11th)
E	
Employee's confinement	(12th from employee-6th)
Employee's hospitalization	(12th from employee-6th)
Employee's secret enemies	(12th from employee-6th)
Employer's death	(8th from employer-10th)

Subject	Derivation
Employer's inheritance	(8th from employer-10th)
Employer's surgery	(8th from employer-10th)
Entertainer	*
Entertainment	*
F	
Family's resources	(2nd from family-4th)
Father's resources	(2nd from father-4th)
Father-in-law's death	(8th from father-in-law-10th)
Father-in-law's inheritance	(8th from father-in-law-10th)
Father-in-law's surgery	(8th from father-in-law-10th)
Fertility	*
Festivals (nonreligious)	*
Fetus	*
Friend's open enemies	(7th from friend-11th)
Friend's partner	(7th from friend-11th)
Friend's spouse	(7th from friend-11th)
G	
Gambler	*
Gambling	*
Games	*
Girlfriend	*
Godchild's open enemies	(7th from godchild-11th)
Godchild's partner	(7th from godchild-11th)
Godchild's spouse	(7th from godchild-11th)
Grandchild's religion	(9th from grandchild-9th)
Grandchild's travel (distant or foreign)	(9th from grandchild-9th)
Grandfather's (paternal) friends	(11th from grandfather-7th)
Grandmother's (maternal) friends	(11th from grandmother-7th)
Gymnasiums	*
H	
Hobby	*
Honeymoon	*
I	
Inventions	*
Investments	*

Subject	Derivation
J	
Jewelry	*
L	
Lotteries	*
Love Affairs	*
Lover	*
M	
Miscarriages	*
Mistresses	*
Mother's death	(8th from mother-10th)
Mother's inheritance	(8th from mother-10th)
Mother's surgery	(8th from mother-10th)
Mother-in-law's resources	(2nd from mother-in-law-4th)
Motion Pictures	*
Movies	*
Music	*
N	
Neighbor's siblings	(3nd from neighbor-3rd)
Neighbor's travel (short distance)	(3nd from neighbor-3rd)
Niece's/Nephew's friends	(11th from niece/nephew-7th
O	
Offspring	*
Open Enemy's friends	(11th from open enemy-7th)
P	
Parent's resources	(2nd from parent-4th)
Parks	*
Parties	*
Partner's friends	(11th from partner-7th)
Pet's confinement	(12th from pet-6th)
Picnics	*
Playgrounds	*
Pleasures	*
Poolrooms	*
Pregnancy	*
Q	
Querent's children	*

Subject	Derivation
R	
Racetracks	*
Raffles	*
Real Estate (profit from)	(2nd from real estate-4th)
Recreation	*
Recreational Vehicles	*
Relationships	*
(romantic, without commitment)	
Resort Area	*
Rodeos	*
Romance	*
S	
Schools (secondary)	*
Secret Enemy's accomplice	(6th from secret-enemy-12th)
Secret Enemy's health/illness	(6th from secret-enemy-12th)
Sex (casual)	*
Show Business	*
Sibling's neighbors	(3rd from sibling-3rd)
Sibling's travel (short distance)	(3rd from sibling-3rd)
Singing	*
Sister-in-law's religion	(9th from sister-in-law-9th)
Sister-in-law's travel	(9th from sister-in-law-9th)
(distant or foreign)	
Son-in-law's	(7th from child-spouse-11th)
open enemies	
Son-in-law's partner	(7th from child-spouse-11th)
Speculation	*
Speculators	*
Sporting Arenas	*
Sporting Events	*
Sports	*
Spouse's friends	(11th from spouse-7th)
Stadiums	*
Stepchild's open enemies	(7th from stepchild-11th)
Stepchild's partner	(7th from stepchild-11th)
Stepchild's spouse	(7th from stepchild-11th)
Stepfather's resources	(2nd from mother-spouse-4th)
Stepmother's death	(8th from father-spouse-10th)
Stepmother's inheritance	(8th from father-spouse-10th)
Stepmother's surgery	(8th from father-spouse-10th)
Stepsibling's career	(10th from mother-spouse-child-8th)

Subject	Derivation
Stepsibling's employer	(10th from mother-spouse-child-8th)
Stepsibling's father	(4th from father-spouse-child-2nd)
Stepsibling's father-in-law	(4th from mother-spouse-child-spouse-2nd)
Stepsibling's mother	(10th from mother-spouse-child--8th)
Stepsibling's mother-in-law	(10th from father-spouse-child-spouse-8th)
Stepsibling's reputation/honor	(10th from mother-spouse-child-8th)
Stepsibling's residence	(4th from father-spouse-child-2nd)
Stepsibling's terminal house	(4th from father-spouse-child-2nd)
Stock Brokers	*
Stocks (as speculation)	*
T	
Taverns	*
Theaters	*
Twins	*
U	
Unborn Child	*
Unborn Child's Sex	*
V	
Vacations	*
Video Games	*
Virginity	*

SIXTH HOUSE

Subject	Derivation
A	
Acupuncture (practitioners of)	*
Air Force	*
Allergies	*
Animal Husbandry	*
Animals (domestic)	*
Animals (large, domestic)	*
Animals (small, domestic)	*
Antibiotics	*
Archives	*
Archivists	*
Armed Services	*
Arms (artificial)	*
Army	*
Artificial Arms	*
Artificial Breast	*
Artificial Eyes	*
Artificial Feet	*
Artificial Hands	*
Artificial Legs	*
Assembly Line	*
Aunt's/Uncle's (maternal) open enemies	(7th from aunt/uncle-12th)
Aunt's/Uncle's (maternal) partner	(7th from aunt/uncle-12th)
Aunt's/Uncle's (maternal) spouse	(7th from aunt/uncle-12th)
Aunts/Uncles (paternal)	(3rd from father-4th)
Aunt's/Uncle's (paternal) physical condition	*
Authority Figure's religion	(9th from authority figure-10th)
Authority Figure's travel (distant or foreign)	(9th from authority figure-10th)
B	
Biofeedback	*
Birds (as pets)	*
Boarders	*
Bookkeepers	*
Breast (artificial)	*

Subject	Derivation
Brother-in-law's career	(10th from brother-in-law-9th)
Brother-in-law's employer	(10th from brother-in-law-9th)
Brother-in-law's father-in-law	(4th from brother-in-law-spouse-3rd)
Brother-in-law's mother	(10th from brother-in-law-9th)
Brother-in-law's reputation/honor	(10th from brother-in-law-9th)
C	
Cafeterias	*
Caretaker	*
Child's (adopted) resources	(2nd from adopted child-5th)
Child's (foster) death	(8th from foster child-11th)
Child's (foster) inheritance	(8th from foster child-11th)
Child's (foster) surgery	(8th from foster child-11th)
Child's resources	(2nd from child-5th)
Chiropodists	*
Chiropractors	*
Civil Service	*
Civil Service Employees	*
Clerks	*
Clothing	*
Commodities	*
Computer Programmers	*
Contact Lenses	*
Cousin's (maternal) neighbors	(3rd from cousin-4th)
Cousin's (maternal) siblings	(3rd from cousin-4th)
Cousin's (maternal) travel (short distance)	(3rd from cousin-4th)
Cousin's (paternal) religion	(9th from cousin-10th)
Cousin's (paternal) travel (distant or foreign)	(9th from cousin-10th)
Co-workers	*
Co-worker's physical condition	*
Craft Associations or Organizations	*
Crafts	*
Craftsmanship	*
D	
Daughter-in-law's death	(8th from child-spouse-11th)
Daughter-in-law's inheritance	(8th from child-spouse-11th)
Daughter-in-law's surgery	(8th from child-spouse-11th)
Dentists	*

Subject	Derivation
Disease	*
Distress	*
Doctors	*
Druggists	*
E	
Employees	*
Employee's physical condition	*
Employees (civil service)	*
Employees (government)	*
Employer's religion	(9th from employer-10th)
Employer's travel (distant or foreign)	(9th from employer-10th)
Employment (in nonautonomous position)	*
Eyeglasses	*
Eyes (artificial)	*
F	
False Teeth	*
Father's neighbors	(3rd from father-4th)
Father's siblings	(3rd from father-4th)
Father's travel (short distance)	(3rd from father-4th)
Father-in-law's religion	(9th from father-in-law-10th)
Father-in-law's travel (distant or foreign)	(9th from father-in-law-10th)
Feet (artificial)	*
Food	*
Food Preparation	*
Food Service	*
Friend's death	(8th from friend-11th)
Friend's inheritance	(8th from friend-11th)
Friend's surgery	(8th from friend-11th)
G	
Godchild's death	(8th from godchild-11th)
Godchild's inheritance	(8th from godchild-11th)
Godchild's surgery	(8th from godchild-11th)
Government Employees	*
Grandchild's career	(10th from grandchild-9th)
Grandchild's employer	(10th from grandchild-9th)
Grandchild's father-in-law	(4th from grandchild-spouse-3rd)
Grandchild's reputation/honor	(10th from grandchild-9th)

Subject	Derivation
Grandfather's (maternal) co-workers	(6th from grandfather-1st)
Grandfather's (maternal) employees	(6th from grandfather-1st)
Grandfather's (maternal) health/illness	(6th from grandfather-1st)
Grandfather's (paternal) confinement	(12th from grandfather-7th)
Grandfather's (paternal) hospitalization	(12th from grandfather-7th)
Grandfather's (paternal) secret enemies	(12th from grandfather-7th)
Grandmother's (maternal) confinement	(12th from grandmother-7th)
Grandmother's (maternal) hospitalization	(12th from grandmother-7th)
Grandmother's (maternal) secret enemies	(12th from grandmother-7th)
Grandmother's (paternal) co-workers	(6th from grandmother-1st)
Grandmother's (paternal) employees	(6th from grandmother-1st)
Grandmother's (paternal) health/illness	(6th from grandmother-1st)
H	
Hands (artificial)	*
Healer	*
Healing	*
Healing (spiritual)	*
Healing Methods	*
Health-aiding Devices	*
Health (querent's)	*
Hearing Aids	*
Horses (domestic)	*
I	
Illness (querent's)	*
Inferiors	*
J	
Job	*
L	
Labor	*
Labor Unions	*
Laborer	*

Subject	Derivation
Legs (artificial)	*
Lessors (tenants)	*
Librarians	*
Lodgers	*
M	
Marine Corps	*
Medication	*
Medicine	*
Military Forces	*
Mother's religion	(9th from mother-10th)
Mother's travel (distant or foreign)	(9th from mother-10th)
Mother-in-law's neighbors	(3rd from mother-in-law-4th)
Mother-in-law's siblings	(3rd from spouse-mother-4th)
Mother-in-law's travel (short distance)	(3rd from mother-in-law-4th)
N	
Navy	*
Neighbor's father	(4th from neighbor-3rd)
Neighbor's mother-in-law	(10th from neighbor-spouse-9th)
Neighbor's residence	(4th from neighbor-3rd)
Neighbor's terminal house	(4th from neighbor-3rd)
Niece's/Nephew's confinement	(12th from niece/nephew-7th)
Niece's/Nephew's hospitalization	(12th from niece/nephew-7th)
Niece's/Nephew's secret enemies	(12th from niece/nephew-7th)
Nurses	*
O	
Occupation	*
Office	*
Open Enemy's confinement	(12th from open enemy-7th)
Open Enemy's hospitalization	(12th from open enemy-7th)
Ophthalmic Devices	*
Orthodontic Devices	*
Orthopedic Devices	*
Others (over whom one has authority)	*
P	
Partner's confinement	(12th from partner-7th)
Partner's hospitalization	(12th from partner-7th)

Subject	Derivation
Partner's secret enemies	(12th from partner-7th)
Peace Corps	*
Pets	*
Pet's physical condition	*
Physical Examinations	*
Physicians	*
Place where business is carried on	*
Programmer (computer)	*
Prosthetic Devices	*
Psychiatrists	*
Q	
Querent's co-workers	*
Querent's employees	*
Querent's health/illness	*
R	
Red Cross	*
Renters (tenants)	*
Repairers	*
Restaurants (as an eating place)	*
S	
Secret Enemy's partner	(7th from secret-enemy-12th)
Secret Enemy's spouse	(7th from secret enemy-12th)
Service	*
Sibling's mother-in-law	(10th from sibling-spouse-9th)
Sibling's residence	(4th from sibling-3rd)
Sibling's terminal house	(4th from sibling-3rd)
Sickness	*
Sister-in-law's career	(10th from sister-in-law-9th)
Sister-in-law's employer	(10th from sister-in-law-9th)
Sister-in-law's father-in-law	(10th from sister-in-law-9th)
Sister-in-law's mother	(10th from sister-in-law-9th)
Sister-in-law's reputation/honor	(10th from sister-in-law-9th)
Son-in-law's death	(8th from child-spouse-11th)
Son-in-law's inheritance	(8th from child-spouse-11th)
Son-in-law's surgery	(8th from child-spouse-11th)
Spouse's aunts/uncles (maternal)	(3rd from spouse-mother-4th)
Spouse's confinement	(12th from spouse-7th)
Spouse's hospitalization	(12th from spouse-7th
Spouse's secret enemies	(12th from spouse-7th)

Subject	Derivation
Stepchild's death	(8th from stepchild-11th)
Stepchild's inheritance	(8th from stepchild-11th)
Stepchild's surgery	(8th from stepchild-11th)
Stepfather's neighbors	(3rd from mother-spouse-4th)
Stepfather's siblings	(3rd from mother-spouse-4th)
Stepfather's travel (short distance)	(3rd from mother-spouse-4th)
Stepmother's religion	(9th from father-spouse-10th)
Stepmother's travel (distant or foreign)	(9th from father-spouse-10th)
Stepsibling's children	(5th from father-spouse-child-2nd)
Stepsibling's friends	(11th from mother-spouse-child-8th)
Strikes (by labor unions)	*
T	
Tenants	*
Trade Unions	*
V	
VISTA (Domestic Peace Corps)	*
Vitamins	*
Volunteer Service	*
W	
Wicker Workers, Caners or Weavers	*
Workers	*
Working Environment	*
Z	
Zoo	*

SEVENTH HOUSE

Subject	Derivation
A	
Adversaries (legal or otherwise)	*
Advisors	*
Agreements	*
Annulments	*
Arbitrator	*
Astrologer (for querent)	*
Audiences	*
Aunt's/Uncle's (maternal) death	(8th from aunt/uncle-12th)
Aunt's/Uncle's (maternal) inheritance	(8th from aunt/uncle-12th)
Aunt's/Uncle's (maternal) surgery	(8th from aunt/uncle-12th)
Aunt's/Uncle's (paternal) resources	(2nd from aunt/uncle-6th)
Authority Figure's career	(10th from authority figure-10th)
Authority Figure's employer	(10th from authority figure-10th)
Authority Figure's father-in-law	(4th from authority figure-spouse-4th)
Authority Figure's mother	(10th from authority figure-10th)
Authority Figure's reputation/honor	(10th from authority figure-10th)
B	
Battles	*
Brother-in-law's friends	(11th from brother-in-law-9th)
Business Associates	*
Buyer or Seller with whom Querent is dealing	*
C	
Child's (adopted) neighbors	(3rd from adopted child-5th)
Child's (adopted) siblings	(3rd from adopted child-5th)
Child's (adopted) travel (short distance)	(3rd from adopted child-5th)
Child's (foster) religion	(9th from foster child-11th)
Child's (foster) travel (distant or foreign)	(9th from foster child-11th)
Child's neighbors	(3rd from child-5th)
Child's travel (short distance)	(3rd from child-5th)
Civil War	*

Subject	Derivation
Client	*
Competition	*
Contests	*
Contractual Relationships	*
Convicts (escaped)	*
Counselor	*
Cousin's (maternal) mother-in-law	(10th from cousin-spouse-10th)
Cousin's (maternal) residence	(4th from cousin-4th)
Cousin's (maternal) terminal house	(4th from cousin-4th)
Cousin's (paternal) career	(10th from cousin-10th)
Cousin's (paternal) employer	(10th from cousin-10th)
Cousin's (paternal) father-in-law	(4th from cousin-spouse-4th)
Cousin's (paternal) reputation/honor	(10th from cousin-10th)
Co-worker's resources	(2nd from co-worker-6th)
Criminal	*
Customer	*

D

Subject	Derivation
Daughter-in-law's religion	(9th from child-spouse-11th)
Daughter-in-law's travel (distant or foreign)	(9th from child-spouse-11th)
Debtor	*
Delegates	*
Delegations	*
Divorce	*
Doctor (querent's)	*
Druggists (querent's)	*

E

Subject	Derivation
Employee's resources	(2nd from employee-6th)
Employer's father-in-law	(4th from employer-spouse-4th)
Employer's mother	(10th from employer-10th)
Employer's reputation/honor	(10th from employer-10th)
Enemy (open)	*

F

Subject	Derivation
Father's residence	(4th from father-4th)
Father's terminal house	(4th from father-4th)
Father-in-law's career	(10th from father-in-law-10th)
Father-in-law's employer	(10th from father-in-law-10th)
Father-in-law's reputation/honor	(10th from father-in-law-10th)
Fiance, Fiancee	*

Subject	Derivation
Friend's religion	(9th from friend-11th)
Friend's travel (distant or foreign)	(9th from friend-11th)
Fugitive	*
G	
Godchild's religion	(9th from godchild-11th)
Godchild's travel (distant or foreign)	(9th from godchild-11th)
Grandchild's friends	(11th from grandchild-9th)
Grandfather (paternal)	(4th from father-4th)
Grandfather's (maternal) open enemies	(7th from grandfather-1st)
Grandfather's (maternal) partner	(7th from grandfather-1st)
Grandfather's (paternal) physical condition	*
Grandmother (maternal)	(10th from mother-10th)
Grandmother's (maternal) physical condition	*
Grandmother's (paternal) open enemies	(7th from grandmother-1st)
Grandmother's (paternal) partner	(7th from grandmother-1st)
H	
Home under consideration (future)	*
Husband	*
L	
Lawyer (querent's)	*
Legal Adversaries	*
M	
Marriage	*
Marriage Partner	*
Mediation	*
Mediator	*
Missing Persons	*
Mother's career	(10th from mother-10th)
Mother's employer	(10th from mother-10th)
Mother's reputation/honor	(10th from mother-10th)
Mother-in-law's residence	(4th from mother-in-law-4th)
Mother-in-law's terminal house	(4th from mother-in-law-4th)

Subject	Derivation
N	
Neighbor's children	(5th from neighbor-3rd)
Nephew (querent's)	(5th from sibling-3rd)
Niece (querent's)	(5th from sibling-3rd)
Niece's/Nephew's physical condition	*
O	
Open Enemy	*
Open Enemy's physical condition	*
Opponent	*
Organ Donors	*
Other People (those not covered by another house)	*
Other Places	*
P	
Partner	*
Partner's physical condition	*
Partnerships	*
Patients	*
Physician (querent's)	*
Public (the)	*
Purchaser	*
Purchasing Agent	*
Q	
Quarrels	*
Querent's open enemies	*
Querent's partner	*
Querent's spouse	*
R	
Relationship (contractual)	*
Relationships (romantic, with commitment)	*
Residence (future, under consideration)	*
Revolution	*
Robber	*
Runaways	*

Subject	Derivation
S	
Secret Enemy's death	(8th from secret-enemy-12th)
Seller or Buyer with whom Querent is dealing	*
Separation	*
Settlements (agreements between people)	*
Shopper	*
Sibling's children	(5th from sibling-3rd)
Sister-in-law's friends	(11th from sister-in-law-9th)
Son-in-law's religion	(9th from child-spouse-11th)
Son-in-law's travel (distant or foreign)	(9th from child-spouse-11th)
Sponsors	*
Spouse	*
Spouse's physical condition	*
Stepchild's religion	(9th from stepchild-11th)
Stepchild's travel (distant or foreign)	(9th from stepchild-11th)
Stepfather's residence	(4th from mother-spouse-4th)
Stepfather's terminal house	(4th from mother-spouse-4th)
Stepmother's career	(10th from father-spouse-10th)
Stepmother's employer	(10th from father-spouse-10th)
Stepmother's reputation/honor	(10th from father-spouse-10th)
Stepsibling's co-workers	(6th from father-spouse-child-2nd)
Stepsibling's confinement	(12th from mother-spouse-child-8th)
Stepsibling's employees	(6th from father-spouse-child-2nd)
Stepsibling's health/illness	(6th from father-spouse-child-2nd)
Stepsibling's hospitalization	(12th from mother-spouse-child-8th)
Stepsibling's secret enemies	(12th from mother-spouse-child-8th)
Strangers	*
Sweethearts	*
T	
Thief	*
W	
War	*
Wife	*

EIGHTH HOUSE

Subject	Derivation
A	
Abortion (surgical)	*
Accountants	*
Accounts	*
Alimony	*
Ammunition	(2nd from war-7th)
Atomic Weapons	(2nd from war-7th)
Audit	*
Aunt's/Uncle's (maternal) religion	(9th from aunt/uncle-12th)
Aunt's/Uncle's (maternal) travel (distant or foreign)	(9th from aunt/uncle-12th)
Aunt's/Uncle's (paternal) neighbors	(3rd from aunt/uncle-6th)
Aunt's/Uncle's (paternal) travel (short distance)	(3rd from aunt/uncle-6th)
Authority Figure's friends	(11th from authority figure-10th)
B	
Bail	*
Bail Bonds	*
Bankruptcy	*
Birth Control	*
Bribery	*
Brothels	*
Brother-in-law's confinement	(12th from brother-in-law-9th)
Brother-in-law's hospitalization	(12th from brother-in-law-9th
Brother-in-law's secret enemies	(12th from brother-in-law-9th)
C	
Castration	*
Caves	*
Cesspools	*
Charge Accounts	*
Child's mother-in-law	(10th from child-spouse-11th)
Child's (adopted) father	(4th from adopted child-5th)
Child's (adopted) mother-in-law	(10th from adopted child-spouse-11th)
Child's (adopted) residence	(4th from adopted child-5th)
Child's (adopted) terminal house	(4th from adopted child-5th)
Child's (foster) career	(10th from foster child-11th)

Subject	Derivation
Child's (foster) employer	(10th from foster child-11th)
Child's (foster) father-in-law	(4th from foster child-spouse-5th)
Child's (foster) mother	(10th from foster child-11th)
Child's (foster) reputation/honor	(10th from foster child-11th)
Child's residence	(4th from child-5th)
Child's terminal house	(4th from child-5th)
Communal Possessions	*
Community Property	*
Compulsion	*
Coroner	*
Cosmetic Surgery	*
Cousin's (maternal) children	(5th from cousin-4th)
Cousin's (paternal) friends	(11th from cousin-10th)
Co-worker's neighbors	(3rd from co-worker-6th)
Co-worker's siblings	(3rd from co-worker-6th)
Co-worker's travel (short distance)	(3rd from co-worker-6th)
Credit	*
Credit Unions	*
Crematories	*
D	
Daughter-in-law's career	(10th from child-spouse-11th)
Daughter-in-law's employer	(10th from child-spouse-11th)
Daughter-in-law's mother	(10th from child-spouse-11th)
Daughter-in-law's reputation/honor	(10th from child-spouse-11th)
Death	*
Debts	*
Detectives	*
Donations	*
Dowry	*
Dreams	*
E	
Employee's neighbors	(3rd from employee-6th)
Employee's siblings	(3rd from employee-6th)
Employee's travel (short distance)	(3rd from employee-6th)
Employer's friends	(11th from employer-10th)
Escrows	*
Estates (inherited)	*
F	
Father-in-law's friends	(11th from father-in-law-10th)

Subject	Derivation
Federal Bureau of Investigation (investigations)	*
Fees	*
Fines	*
Friend's career	(10th from friend-11th)
Friend's employer	(10th from friend-11th)
Friend's father-in-law	(4th from friend-spouse-5th)
Friend's mother	(10th from friend-11th)
Friend's reputation/honor	(10th from friend-11th)
G	
Gifts (received from others)	*
Godchild's career	(10th from godchild-11th)
Godchild's employer	(10th from godchild-11th)
Godchild's father-in-law	(4th from godchild-spouse-5th)
Godchild's mother	(10th from godchild-11th)
Godchild's reputation/honor	(10th from godchild-11th)
Grandchild's confinement	(12th from grandchild-9th)
Grandchild's hospitalization	(12th from grandchild-9th)
Grandchild's secret enemies	(12th from grandchild-9th)
Grandfather's (maternal) death	(8th from grandfather-1st)
Grandfather's (maternal) inheritance	(8th from grandfather-1st)
Grandfather's (maternal) surgery	(8th from grandfather-1st)
Grandfather's (paternal) resources	(2nd from grandfather-7th)
Grandmother's (maternal) resources	(2nd from grandmother-7th)
Grandmother's (paternal) death	(8th from grandmother-1st)
Grandmother's (paternal) inheritance	(8th from grandmother-1st)
Grandmother's (paternal) surgery	(8th from grandmother-1st)
Grants	*
Gratuities	*
H	
Hair Transplants	*
Hysterectomy	*
I	
Inheritance (querent's)	*
Inquests	*
Insects	*
Installment Buying	*
Insurance (as beneficiary)	*
Insurance (querent's)	*

Subject	Derivation
Insurance (unemployment)	*
Insurance Proceeds	*
Internal Revenue Service Tax Audit	*
J	
Joint Savings	*
L	
Latrines	*
Legacy	*
Lending Agencies	*
Loan Companies	*
Loans	*
M	
Martial Arts	*
Medicaid	*
Medicare	*
Money (owed to others)	*
Money Market Funds	*
Mortgage Companies	*
Mortgages	*
Mother's friends	(11th from mother-10th)
N	
Neighbor's co-workers	(6th from neighbor-3rd)
Neighbor's employees	(6th from neighbor-3rd)
Neighbor's health/illness	(6th from neighbor-3rd)
Niece's/Nephew's resources	(2nd from niece/nephew-7th)
Nuclear Weapons	(2nd from war-7th)
O	
Obsession	*
Occultism	*
Omens	*
Open Enemy's resources	(2nd from open enemy-7th)
Organ Transplants	*
Organized Crime	*
P	
Palimony	*
Pall Bearers	*

Subject	Derivation
Partner's resources	(2nd from partner-7th)
Pension Funds	*
Plastic Surgery	*
Possessions (communal)	*
Possessions (joint)	*
Profit Sharing Plans	*
Prostitutes	*
Public Funds	*
Q	
Querent's inheritance	*
Querent's surgery	*
R	
Research	*
Resources (joint)	*
Retirement Funds	*
Retirement Plans	*
S	
Savings (joint)	*
Secret Enemy's religion	(9th from secret-enemy-12th)
Septic Tanks	*
Settlements (financial)	*
Sewage Systems	*
Sewers	*
Sex (with commitment)	*
Sibling's co-workers	(6th from sibling-3rd)
Sibling's employees	(6th from sibling-3rd)
Sibling's health/illness	(6th from sibling-3rd)
Sister-in-law's confinement	(12th from sister-in-law-9th)
Sister-in-law's hospitalization	(12th from sister-in-law-9th
Sister-in-law's secret enemies	(12th from sister-in-law-9th)
Social Security	*
Son-in-law's career	(10th from child-spouse-11th)
Son-in-law's employer	(10th from child-spouse-11th)
Son-in-law's mother	(10th from child-spouse-11th)
Son-in-law's reputation/honor	(10th from child-spouse-11th)
Spouse's resources	(2nd from spouse-7th)
Stepchild's career	(10th from stepchild-11th)
Stepchild's employer	(10th from stepchild-11th)
Stepchild's father-in-law	(4th from stepchild-spouse-5th)

Subject	Derivation
Stepchild's mother	(10th from stepchild-11th)
Stepchild's reputation/honor	(10th from stepchild-11th)
Stepmother's friends	(11th from father-spouse-10th)
Stepsibling (Mother's step-child)	(5th from mother-spouse-4th)
Stepsibling's open enemies	(7th from father-spouse-child-2nd)
Stepsibling's partner	(7th from father-spouse-child-2nd)
Stepsibling's physical condition	*
Stepsibling's spouse	(7th from father-spouse-child-2nd)
Sterilization (sexual)	*
Surgeons	*
Surgery	*
T	
Tax Assessors	*
Tax Audit	*
Tax Collector	*
Tax Consultants	*
Taxes	*
Tips/Gratuities	*
Toilets	*
Trust Funds	*
Tubal Ligation	*
U	
Undertaker	*
Underworld	*
Unemployment Compensation	*
V	
Vasectomy	*
Victim (murder)	*
W	
Weapons of War	(2nd from war-7th)
Wills	*
Workers Compensation	*

NINTH HOUSE

Subject	Derivation
A	
Advertising Agencies	*
Agents (travel)	*
Aircraft	*
Airline Steward/Stewardess	*
Airports	*
Aliens	*
Archbishops	*
Astral Travel	*
Astrology	*
Aunt's/Uncle's (maternal) career	(10th from aunt/uncle-12th)
Aunt's/Uncle's (maternal) employer	(10th from aunt/uncle-12th)
Aunt's/Uncle's (maternal) father-in-law	(4th from aunt/uncle-spouse-6th)
Aunt's/Uncle's (maternal) reputation/honor	(10th from aunt/uncle-12th)
Aunt's/Uncle's (paternal) mother-in-law	(10th from aunt/uncle-spouse-12th)
Aunt's/Uncle's (paternal) residence	(4th from aunt/uncle-6th)
Aunt's/Uncle's (paternal) terminal house	(4th from aunt/uncle-6th)
Authority Figure's confinement	(12th from authority figure-10th)
Authority Figure's hospitalization	(12th from authority figure-10th)
Authority Figure's secret enemies	(12th from authority figure-10th)
B	
Baptism	*
Bar mitzvah	*
Bas mitzvah	*
Bishops	*
Brother-in-law	(3rd from spouse-7th, or 7th from sibling-3rd)
Brother-in-law's physical condition	*
C	
Ceremony (religious)	*
Chapels	*
Child's (adopted) children	(5th from adopted child-5th)
Child's (foster) friends	(11th from foster child-11th)

Subject	Derivation
Churches	*
Clergy	*
Clergymen/Clergywomen	*
College Major (area of study)	*
Comets	*
Consulate	*
Coronations	*
Corporation	*
Court System	*
Cousin's (maternal) co-workers	(6th from cousin-4th)
Cousin's (maternal) employees	(6th from cousin-4th)
Cousin's (maternal) health/illness	(6th from cousin-4th)
Cousin's (paternal) confinement	(12th from cousin-10th)
Cousin's (paternal) hospitalization	(12th from cousin-10th)
Cousin's (paternal) secret enemies	(12th from cousin-10th)
Co-worker's father	(4th from co-worker-6th)
Co-worker's mother-in-law	(10th from co-worker-spouse-12th)
Co-worker's residence	(4th from co-worker-6th)
Co-worker's terminal house	(4th from co-worker-6th)

D

Subject	Derivation
Daughter-in-law's friends	(11th from child-spouse-11th)
Deacons	*

E

Subject	Derivation
Education (higher)	*
Employee's father	(4th from employee-6th)
Employee's mother-in-law	(10th from employee-spouse-12th)
Employee's residence	(4th from employee-6th)
Employee's terminal house	(4th from employee-6th)
Employer's confinement	(12th from employer-10th)
Employer's hospitalization	(12th from employer-10th)
Employer's secret enemies	(12th from employer-10th)
Explorers	*
Extra-terrestrials	*

F

Subject	Derivation
Father's co-workers	(6th from father-4th)
Father's employees	(6th from father-4th)
Father's health/illness	(6th from father-4th)
Father-in-law's confinement	(12th from father-in-law-10th)
Father-in-law's hospitalization	(12th from father-in-law-10th)

Subject	Derivation
Father-in-law's secret enemies	(12th from father-in-law-10th)
Festivals (religious)	*
Flight Attendants	*
Foreign Countries	*
Foreigners	*
Friend's friends	(11th from friend-11th)
Funeral Ceremony	*

G

Subject	Derivation
Godchild's friends	(11th from godchild-11th)
Grandchild/grandchildren	(5th from child-5th)
Grandchild's physical condition	*
Grandfather's (maternal) religion	(9th from grandfather-1st)
Grandfather's (maternal) travel (distant or foreign)	(9th from grandfather-1st)
Grandfather's (paternal) neighbors	(3rd from grandfather-7th)
Grandfather's (paternal) siblings	(3rd from grandfather-7th)
Grandfather's (paternal) travel (short distance)	(3rd from grandfather-7th)
Grandmother's (maternal) neighbors	(3rd from grandmother-7th)
Grandmother's (maternal) siblings	(3rd from grandmother-7th)
Grandmother's (maternal) travel (short distance)	(3rd from grandmother-7th)
Grandmother's (paternal) religion	(9th from grandmother-1st)
Grandmother's (paternal) travel (distant or foreign)	(9th from grandmother-1st)
Guru	*

H

Subject	Derivation
Host/Hostess (airline)	*
Hymns	*

I

Subject	Derivation
Inaugurations	*
In-laws (brother)	(3rd from spouse-7th, or 7th from sibling-3rd)
In-laws (sister)	(3rd from spouse-7th, or 7th from sibling-3rd)
Insurance Adjustors	*
Insurance Company (as a corporation)	*

Subject	Derivation
J	
Journeys	*
Judicial System	*
L	
Lawsuits	*
Lawyers (in a court case)	*
M	
Metaphysics	*
Meteorite	*
Ministers	*
Mother's confinement	(12th from mother-10th)
Mother's hospitalization	(12th from mother-10th)
Mother's secret enemies	(12th from mother-10th)
Mother-in-law's co-workers	(6th from mother-in-law-4th)
Mother-in-law's employees	(6th from mother-in-law-4th)
Mother-in-law's health/illness	(6th from mother-in-law-4th)
N	
Neighbor's open enemies	(7th from neighbor-3rd)
Neighbor's partner	(7th from neighbor-3rd)
Neighbor's spouse	(7th from neighbor-3rd)
Niece's/Nephew's neighbors	(3rd from niece/nephew7th)
Niece's/Nephew's travel (short distance)	(3rd from niece/nephew-7th)
Nuns	*
O	
Open Enemy's siblings	(3rd from open enemy-7th)
P	
Parades	*
Partner's neighbors	(3rd from partner-7th)
Partner's siblings	(3rd from partner-7th)
Partner's travel (short distance)	(3rd from partner-7th)
Pet's terminal house	(4th from pet-6th)
Philanthropists	*
Philosophers	*
Philosophy	*
Pilots	*
Prayers	*

Subject	Derivation
Preachers	*
Priests	*
Publisher	*
Publishing	*
Q	
Querent's religion	*
Querent's travel (distance or foreign)	*
R	
Rabbis	*
Religion	*
Religious Ceremony	*
Religious Sects	*
Ritual (religious)	*
S	
Satellites	*
Schools (higher education)	*
Science	*
Secret Enemy's career	(10th from secret-enemy-12th)
Secret Enemy's employer	(10th from secret-enemy-12th)
Secret Enemy's reputation/honor	(10th from secret-enemy-12th)
Sects (religious)	*
Shrines	*
Sibling's open enemies	(7th from sibling-3rd)
Sibling's partner	(7th from sibling-3rd)
Sister-in-law	(3rd from spouse-7th, or 7th from sibling-3rd)
Sister-in-law's physical condition	*
Son-in-law's friends	(11th from child-spouse-11th)
Space Travel	*
Spouse's travel (short distance)	(3rd from spouse-7th)
Stepchild's friends	(11th from stepchild-11th)
Stepfather's co-workers	(6th from mother-spouse-4th)
Stepfather's employees	(6th from mother-spouse-4th)
Stepfather's health/illness	(6th from mother-spouse-4th)
Stepmother's confinement	(12th from father-spouse-10th)
Stepmother's hospitalization	(12th from father-spouse-10th)
Stepmother's secret enemies	(12th from father-spouse-10th)
Stepsibling's death	(8th from father-spouse-child-2nd)
Stepsibling's inheritance	(8th from father-spouse-child-2nd)

Subject	Derivation
Stepsibling's resources	(2nd from mother-spouse-child-8th)
Stepsibling's surgery	(8th from father-spouse-child-2nd)
Steward/Stewardess (airline)	*
Supreme Court	*
Synagogues	*
T	
Temples	*
Travel (long distance, duration, or foreign)	*
Travel (space)	*
Travel Agents	*
Travelers	*
V	
Vehicles of War	(3rd from war-7th)
Visions	*
W	
Wedding	*

TENTH HOUSE

Subject	Derivation
A	
Achievements	*
Administration	*
Administrators	*
Auctions	*
Aunt's/Uncle's (maternal) friends	(11th from aunt/uncle-12th)
Authority Figures	*
Authority Symbols	*
Authority Figure's physical condition	*
Awards	*
B	
Brother-in-law's resources	(2nd from brother-in-law-9th)
Businesses	*
C	
Career (querent's)	*
Child's (adopted) co-workers	(6th from adopted child-5th)
Child's (adopted) employees	(6th from adopted child-5th)
Child's (adopted) health/illness	(6th from adopted child-5th)
Child's (foster) confinement	(12th from foster child-11th)
Child's (foster) hospitalization	(12th from foster child-11th)
Child's (foster) secret enemies	(12th from foster child-11th)
Child's co-workers	(6th from child-5th)
Child's employees	(6th from child-5th)
Child's health/illness	(6th from child-5th)
City Hall	*
Committee	*
(for a political entity)	
Corporation's profit or money	(2nd from corporation-9th)
Council members	*
Courthouse	*
Cousin (paternal)	(5th from aunt/uncle-6th)
Cousin's (maternal) open enemies	(7th from cousin-4th)
Cousin's (maternal) partner	(7th from cousin-4th)
Cousin's (maternal) spouse	(7th from cousin-4th)
Cousin's (paternal)	*
physical condition	
Co-worker's children	(5th from co-worker-6th)

Subject	Derivation
D	
Daughter-in-law's confinement	(12th from child-spouse-11th)
Daughter-in-law's hospitalization	(12th from child-spouse-11th)
Daughter-in-law's secret enemies	(12th from child-spouse-11th)
Dictatorships	*
E	
Electric Company	*
Employee's children	(5th from employee-6th)
Employers	*
Employer's physical condition	*
Employment	
(in authoritative position)	*
Executives	*
F	
Fame	*
Father's open enemies	(7th from father-4th)
Father's partner	(7th from father-4th)
Father-in-law	(4th from spouse-7th)
Father-in-law's physical condition	*
Federal Bureau of Investigation	
(Govt. Agency)	*
Flea Markets	*
Franchises	*
Friend's confinement	(12th from friend-11th)
Friend's hospitalization	(12th from friend-11th)
Friend's secret enemies	(12th from friend-11th)
G	
Gas Company	*
Godchild's confinement	(12th from godchild-11th)
Godchild's hospitalization	(12th from godchild-11th)
Godchild's secret enemies	(12th from godchild-11th)
Government	*
Government Agencies	*
Government Programs	*
Governor	*
Grandchild's resources	(2nd from grandchild-9th)
Grandfather's (maternal) career	(10th from grandfather-1st)
Grandfather's (maternal) employer	(10th from grandfather-1st)

Subject	Derivation
Grandfather's (maternal) reputation/honor	(10th from grandfather-1st)
Grandfather's (paternal) residence	(4th from grandfather-7th)
Grandfather's (paternal) terminal house	(4th from grandfather-7th)
Grandmother's (maternal) residence	(4th from grandmother-7th)
Grandmother's (maternal) terminal house	(4th from grandmother-7th)
Grandmother's (paternal) career	(10th from grandmother-1st)
Grandmother's (paternal) reputation/honor	(10th from grandmother-1st)
Guardian (querent's)	*
H	
Heads of State	*
Honor	*
Honor (querent's)	*
I	
In-law (father)	(4th from spouse-7th)
Internal Revenue Service (Govt. Agency)	*
J	
Judges	*
L	
Landlord	*
Law Enforcement	*
Leaders	*
M	
Magistrates	*
Management	*
Mayor	*
Mother	*
Mother's physical condition	*
Mother-in-law's open enemies	(7th from mother-in-law-4th)
Mother-in-law's partner	(7th from mother-in-law-4th)
N	
Neighbor's death	(8th from neighbor-3rd)

Subject	Derivation
Neighbor's inheritance	(8th from neighbor-3rd)
Neighbor's surgery	(8th from neighbor-3rd)
Niece's/Nephew's father	(4th from niece/nephew-7th)
Niece's/Nephew's mother-in-law	(10 from niece/nephew-spouse-1st)
Niece's/Nephew's residence	(4th from niece/nephew-7th)
Niece's/Nephew's terminal house	(4th from niece/nephew-7th)
Notoriety	*
O	
Open Enemy's residence	(4th from open enemy-7th)
Open Enemy's terminal house	(4th from open enemy-7th)
P	
Parliament	*
Partner's father	(4th from partner-7th)
Partner's mother-in-law	(10th from partner-spouse-1st)
Partner's residence	(4th from partner-7th)
Partner's terminal house	(4th from partner-7th)
Police	*
Police Officers	*
Political Party (in power)	*
Politicians	*
Pope	*
Power	*
President	*
Profession (querent's)	*
Professionals	*
Profit (from corporation)	(2nd from corporation-9th)
Profit (from publication)	(2nd from publication-9th)
Profit (from travel)	(2nd from travel-9th)
Promotion (career)	*
Public Status (querent's)	*
Publicity	*
Q	
Querent's career	(4th from spouse-7th)
Querent's employer	(4th from spouse-7th)
Querent's father-in-law	(4th from spouse-7th)
Querent's mother	(4th from spouse-7th)
Querent's reputation/honor	(4th from spouse-7th)

Subject	Derivation
R	
Rank	*
Representatives	*
Reputation	*
Restaurants (as a business)	*
Royalty	*
Rulers (of countries)	*
S	
Scandal	*
Secret Enemy's friends	(11th from secret-enemy-12th)
Selectmen (town officers)	*
Senators	*
Sheriffs	'*
Sibling's death	(8th from sibling-3rd)
Sibling's inheritance	(8th from sibling-3rd)
Sibling's surgery	(8th from sibling-3rd)
Sister-in-law's resources	(2nd from sister-in-law-9th)
Son-in-law's confinement	(12th from child-spouse-11th)
Son-in-law's hospitalization	(12th from child-spouse-11th)
Son-in-law's secret enemies	(12th from child-spouse-11th)
Spouse's terminal house	(4th from spouse-7th)
Status	*
Stepchild's confinement	(12th from stepchild-11th)
Stepchild's hospitalization	(12th from stepchild-11th)
Stepchild's secret enemies	(12th from stepchild-11th)
Stepfather's open enemies	(7th from mother-spouse-4th)
Stepfather's partner	(7th from mother-spouse-4th)
Stepmother	(7th from father-4th)
Stepmother's physical condition	*
Stepsibling's neighbors	(3rd from mother-spouse-child-8th)
Stepsibling's religion	(9th from father-spouse-child-2nd)
Stepsibling's siblings	(3rd from mother-spouse-child-8th)
Stepsibling's travel (distant or foreign)	(9th from father-spouse-child-2nd)
Stepsibling's travel (short distance)	(3rd from mother-spouse-child-8th)
Superiors	*
Supervisors	*
T	
Telephone Company	*
Town Hall	*

Subject	Derivation
U Utility Company	*

ELEVENTH HOUSE

Subject	Derivation
A	
Acquaintances	*
Alderman	*
Ambassadors to (other countries)	*
Associations (fraternal)	*
Aunt's/Uncle's (maternal) confinement	(12th from aunt/uncle-12th)
Aunt's/Uncle's (maternal) hospitalization	(12th from aunt/uncle-12th)
Aunt's/Uncle's (maternal) secret enemies	(12th from aunt/uncle-12th)
Aunt's/Uncle's (paternal) co-workers	(6th from aunt/uncle-6th)
Aunt's/Uncle's (paternal) employees	(6th from aunt/uncle-6th)
Aunt's/Uncle's (paternal) health/illness	(6th from aunt/uncle-6th)
Authority Figure's resources	(2nd from authority figure-10th)
B	
Brother-in-law's neighbors	(3rd from brother-in-law-9th)
Brother-in-law's siblings	(3rd from brother-in-law-9th)
Brother-in-law's travel (short distance)	(3rd from brother-in-law-9th)
Business Profits	(2nd from business-10th)
C	
Chamber of Commerce	*
Child (foster)	(5th from other-7th)
Child (step)	(5th from spouse-7th)
Child's (adopted) open enemies	(7th from adopted child-5th)
Child's (adopted) partner	(7th from adopted child-5th)
Child's (adopted) spouse	(7th from adopted child-5th)
Child's (foster) physical condition	*
Child's open enemies	(7th from child-5th)
Child's partner	(7th from child-5th)
Child's spouse	(7th from child-5th)
Club Members	*
Clubs	*
Committee (for a fraternal group)	*
Commodity Exchange	*

Subject	Derivation
Congress	*
Congressmen	*
Conventions	*
Cousin's (maternal) death	(8th from cousin-4th)
Cousin's (maternal) inheritance	(8th from cousin-4th)
Cousin's (maternal) surgery	(8th from cousin-4th)
Cousin's (paternal) resources	(2nd from cousin-10th)
Co-worker's employees	(6th from co-worker-6th)
Co-worker's health/illness	(6th from co-worker-6th)
D	
Daughter-in-law	(7th from child-5th)
Daughter-in-law's physical condition	*
Deaths in the family	(8th from family-4th)
E	
Employee's health/illness	(6th from employee-6th)
Employer's resources	(2nd from employer-10th)
F	
Father's death	(8th from father-4th)
Father's inheritance	(8th from father-4th)
Father's surgery	(8th from father-4th)
Father-in-law's resources	(2nd from father-in-law-10th)
Foster Child	(5th from other-7th)
Fraternal Groups/Clubs/ Organizations	*
Friends	*
Friend's physical condition	*
G	
Goals	*
Godchild	(5th from other-7th)
Godchild's physical condition	*
Grandchild's neighbors	(3rd from grandchild-9th)
Grandchild's siblings	(3rd from grandchild-9th)
Grandchild's travel (short distance)	(3rd from grandchild-9th)
Grandfather's (maternal) friends	(11th from grandfather-1st)
Grandmother's (paternal) friends	(11th from grandmother-1st)
Groups	*

Subject	Derivation
H	
Hopes	*
House of Commons	*
House of Representatives	*
J	
Jury	*
L	
Legislators	*
Lodges (fraternal)	*
M	
Money (from business)	(2nd from business-10th)
Mother's resources	(2nd from mother-10th)
Mother-in-law's death	(8th from mother-in-law-4th)
Mother-in-law's inheritance	(8th from mother-in-law-4th)
Mother-in-law's surgery	(8th from mother-in-law-4th)
N	
Neighbor's religion	(9th from neighbor-3rd)
Neighbor's travel (distant or foreign)	(9th from neighbor-3rd)
Niece's/Nephew's children	(5th from niece/nephew-7th)
O	
Open Enemy's children	(5th from open enemy-7th)
Organizations	*
Organized Charities	*
P	
Partner's children	(5th from partner-7th)
Pet's health/illness	(6th from pet-6th)
Platonic Relationships	*
Profit (from business)	(2nd from business-10th)
Q	
Querent's friends	*
R	
Radiation Therapy	(6th from physician-6th)

Subject	Derivation
S	
Secret Enemy's confinement	(12th from secret-enemy-12th)
Secret Enemy's hospitalization	(12th from secret-enemy-12th)
Senate	*
Sibling's religion	(9th from sibling-3rd)
Sibling's travel (distant or foreign)	(9th from sibling-3rd)
Sister-in-law's neighbors	(3rd from sister-in-law-9th)
Sister-in-law's siblings	(3rd from sister-in-law-9th)
Sister-in-law's travel (short distance)	(3rd from sister-in-law-9th)
Societies (fraternal)	*
Son-in-law	(7th from child-5th)
Son-in-law's physical condition	*
Stepchild	(5th from spouse-7th)
Stepchild's physical condition	*
Stepfather's death	(8th from mother-spouse-4th)
Stepfather's inheritance	(8th from mother-spouse-4th)
Stepfather's surgery	(8th from mother-spouse-4th)
Stepmother's resources	(2nd from father-spouse-10th)
Stepsibling's career	(10th from father-spouse-child-2nd)
Stepsibling's employer	(10th from father-spouse-child-2nd)
Stepsibling's father-in-law	(4th from father-spouse-child-spouse-8th)
Stepsibling's mother-in-law	(10th from mother-spouse-child-spouse-2nd)
Stepsibling's reputation/honor	(10th from father-spouse-child-2nd)
Stepsibling's residence	(4th from mother-spouse-child-8th)
Stepsibling's terminal house	(4th from mother-spouse-child-8th)
Stock Exchange	*
U	
Utility Meters	*
W	
Wishes	*
Women's liberation organizations	*
X	
X-rays	(6th from physician-6th)

TWELFTH HOUSE

Subject	Derivation
A	
Abbeys	*
Ambushes	*
Ancients	*
Animals (large, wild)	*
Animals (small, wild)	*
Animals (wild)	*
Ashrams	*
Assassination	*
Assassins	*
Astral Entities	*
Asylums	*
Attacker	*
Aunt/Uncle (maternal)	(3rd from mother-10th)
Aunt's/Uncle's (maternal) physical condition	*
Aunt's/Uncle's (paternal) open enemies	(7th from aunt/uncle-6th)
Aunt's/Uncle's (paternal) partner	(7th from aunt/uncle-6th)
Aunt's/Uncle's (paternal) spouse	(7th from aunt/uncle-6th)
Authority Figure's neighbors	(3rd from authority figure-10th)
Authority Figure's siblings	(3rd from authority figure-10th)
Authority Figure's travel short distance	(3rd from authority figure-10th)
B	
Bereavement	*
Birds (wild)	*
Blackmail	*
Bondage	*
Brother-in-law's father	(4th from brother-in-law-9th)
Brother-in-law's mother-in-law	(10th from brother-in-law-spouse-3rd)
Brother-in-law's residence	(4th from brother-in-law-9th)
Brother-in-law's terminal house	(4th from brother-in-law-9th)
Burglars	*
Burglary	*
Business Locality	(3rd from business-10th)

Subject	Derivation
C	
Captivity (place of)	*
Cattle	*
Charities	*
Charity Recipients	*
Child's (adopted) death	(8th from adopted child-5th)
Child's (adopted) inheritance	(8th from adopted child-5th)
Child's (adopted) surgery	(8th from adopted child-5th)
Child's (foster) resources	(2nd from foster child-11th)
Child's death	(8th from child-5th)
Child's inheritance	(8th from child-5th)
Child's surgery	(8th from child-5th)
Clandestine Associates	*
Clandestine Matters	*
Clinics (medical)	*
Cloisters	*
Cloisters (convents)	*
Concentration Camps	*
Confinement	*
Convents	*
Cousin's (maternal) religion	(9th from cousin-4th)
Cousin's (maternal) travel (distant or foreign)	(9th from cousin-4th)
Cousin's (paternal) neighbors	(3rd from cousin-10th)
Cousin's (paternal) siblings	(3rd from cousin-10th)
Cousin's (paternal) travel (short distance)	(3rd from cousin-10th)
Co-worker's open enemies	(7th from co-worker-6th)
Co-worker's partner	(7th from co-worker-6th)
Co-worker's spouse	(7th from co-worker-6th)
D	
Daughter-in-law's resources	(2nd from child-spouse-11th)
Detention (places of)	*
Doctor's office/clinic	(6th from doctor-7th)
Drug Addiction	*
Drug Rehabilitation Center	*
Drugs (habit forming)	*
Drugs (illegal)	*
E	
Employee's open enemies	(7th from employee-6th)

Subject	Derivation
Employee's partner	(7th from employee-6th)
Employer's neighbors	(3rd from employer-10th)
Employer's siblings	(3rd from employer-10th)
Employer's travel (short distance)	(3rd from employer-10th)
Enemy (secret)	*
Exile	*
F	
Father's religion	(9th from father-4th)
Father's travel (distant or foreign)	(9th from father-4th)
Father-in-law's neighbors	(3rd from father-in-law-10th)
Father-in-law's siblings	(3rd from spouse-father-10th)
Father-in-law's travel (short distance)	(3rd from father-in-law-10th)
Food Stamp Recipients	*
Friend's resources	(2nd from friend-11th)
G	
Ghettos	*
Ghost Towns	*
Ghosts	*
Godchild's resources	(2nd from godchild-11th)
Government Agencies (secret)	*
Grandchild's mother-in-law	(10th from grandchild-spouse-3rd)
Grandchild's residence	(4th from grandchild-9th)
Grandchild's terminal house	(4th from grandchild-9th)
Grandfather's (maternal) confinement	(12th from grandfather-1st)
Grandfather's (maternal) hospitalization	(12th from grandfather-1st)
Grandfather's (maternal) secret enemies	(12th from grandfather-1st)
Grandfather's (paternal) co-workers	(6th from grandfather-7th)
Grandfather's (paternal) employees	(6th from grandfather-7th)
Grandfather's (paternal) health/illness	(6th from grandfather-7th)
Grandmother's (maternal) co-workers	(6th from grandmother-7th)
Grandmother's (maternal) employees	(6th from grandmother-7th)
Grandmother's (maternal) health/illness	(6th from grandmother-7th)
Grandmother's (paternal) confinement	(12th from grandmother-1st)

Subject	Derivation
Grandmother's (paternal) hospitalization	(12th from grandmother-1st)
Grandmother's (paternal) secret enemies	(12th from grandmother-1st)
Guard	*
H	
Hidden Things	*
Horses (wild)	*
Hospitalization	*
Hospitals	*
I	
Imprisonment	*
Informer	*
Institutions	*
Internment Camps	*
J	
Jailers (keeper)	*
Jails	*
K	
Kidnap	*
Kidnapper	*
M	
Matron of Jail	*
Monasteries	*
Monk	*
Mother's neighbors	(3rd from mother-10th)
Mother's siblings	(3rd from mother-10th)
Mother's travel (short distance)	(3rd from mother-10th)
Mother-in-law's religion	(9th from mother-in-law-4th)
Mother-in-law's travel (distant or foreign)	(9th from mother-in-law-4th)
Motives (hidden, of accuser)	*
Murder	*
N	
Narcotics	*
Neighbor's career	(10th from neighbor-3rd)

Subject	Derivation
Neighbor's employer	(10th from neighbor-3rd)
Neighbor's father-in-law	(4th from neighbor-spouse-9th)
Neighbor's mother	(10th from neighbor-3rd)
Neighbor's reputation/honor	(10th from neighbor-3rd)
Niece's/Nephew's co-workers	(6th from niece/nephew-7th)
Niece's/Nephew's employees	(6th from niece/nephew-7th)
Niece's/Nephew's health/illness	(6th from niece/nephew-7th)
Nuns (cloistered)	*
Nursing Homes	*
O	
Oil	*
Oil Wells	*
Open Enemy's accomplice	(6th from open enemy-7th)
Open Enemy's health	(6th from open enemy-7th)
Orphans	*
P	
Partner's co-workers	(6th from partner-7th)
Partner's employees	(6th from partner-7th)
Partner's health/illness	(6th from partner-7th)
Persecutor	*
Perverts	*
Places (secluded or remote)	*
Poisons	*
Possession (by entities)	*
Prison Farms	*
Prisoner of War Camps	*
Prisons	*
Psychic abilities	*
Psychosis	*
Q	
Querent's confinement	*
Querent's hospitalization	*
Querent's secret enemies	*
R	
Rapist	*
Recluse	*
Reform Schools	*
Reformatories	*

Subject	Derivation
Refugee Camps	*
Remote Places	*
Rest Home	*
Retirement	*
Retreat (places of)	*
S	
Sanitarium	*
Secluded Places	*
Seclusion	*
Secret Enemy	*
Secret Enemy's physical condition	*
Secret Service	*
Secret Societies	*
Self Destruction	*
Self Undoing	*
Sibling's career	(10th from sibling-3rd)
Sibling's employer	(10th from sibling-3rd)
Sibling's father-in-law	(4th from sibling-spouse-9th)
Sibling's reputation/honor	(10th from sibling-3rd)
Sister-in-law's father	(4th from sister-in-law-9th)
Sister-in-law's mother-in-law	(10th from sister-in-law-spouse-3rd)
Sister-in-law's residence	(4th from sister-in-law-9th)
Sister-in-law's terminal house	(4th from sister-in-law-9th)
Slavery	*
Sleep	*
Son-in-law's resources	(2nd from child-spouse-11th)
Spies	*
Spouse's aunts/uncles (paternal)	(3rd from spouse-father-10th)
Spouse's co-workers	(6th from spouse-7th)
Spouse's employees	(6th from spouse-7th)
Spouse's health/illness	(6th from spouse-7th)
Stepchild's resources	(2nd from stepchild-11th)
Stepfather's religion	(9th from mother-spouse-4th)
Stepfather's travel (distant or foreign)	(9th from mother-spouse-4th)
Stepmother's neighbors	(3rd from father-spouse-10th)
Stepmother's siblings	(3rd from father-spouse-10th)
Stepmother's travel (short distance)	(3rd from father-spouse-10th)
Stepsibling's children	(5th from mother-spouse-child-8th)
Stepsibling's friends	(11th from father-spouse-child-2nd)
Subversion	*

Subject	Derivation
Suicide	*
T	
Terrorists	*
Treason	*
V	
Veterinarians	(6th from pet-6th)
W	
Warden of Jail	*
Welfare Recipients	*
Widows	*
Y	
Yesterday	*

PART VI

PARTS OF THE BODY

Part of Body	Ruling Sign	Ruling Planet
A		
Abdominal Cavity	♍ Virgo	
Adenoids	♉ Taurus	
Adrenal Glands	♎ Libra	♂ Mars
Alimentary Canal	♋ Cancer	
Ankles	♒ Aquarius	
Aorta	♌ Leo	
Appendix	♏ Scorpio	♇ Pluto
Arms	♊ Gemini	☿ Mercury
Arterial Blood System	♐ Sagittarius	♃ Jupiter
B		
Back (Lower)	♎ Libra	
Back (Upper)	♌ Leo	☉ Sun
Bile	♐ Sagittarius	
Bladder	♎ Libra	
Blood	♐ Sagittarius	♃ Jupiter
Blood Circulation	♒ Aquarius	♅ Uranus
Blood Plasma		☽ Moon
Body Metabolism	♍ Virgo	
Body Minerals	♑ Capricorn	
Bone Marrow	♑ Capricorn	♄ Saturn
Bones	♑ Capricorn	♄ Saturn
Brain	♈ Aries	☽ Moon
Breast	♋ Cancer	
Breath	♊ Gemini	
Breathing Apparatus	♊ Gemini	
Bronchi	♊ Gemini	
Buttocks	♐ Sagittarius	
C		
Capillaries	♊ Gemini	
Cerebellum (Lower Brain)	♉ Taurus	
Cerebrum (Upper Brain)	♈ Aries	
Colon	♏ Scorpio	
D		
Diaphragm	♊ Gemini	
Digestive System	♍ Virgo	☿ Mercury
E		
Ears		♄ Saturn

Part of Body	Ruling Sign	Ruling Planet
Eliminative Channels	♏ Scorpio	♇ Pluto
Endocrine System	♓ Pisces	♆ Neptune
Equilibrium	♎ Libra	
Esophagus	♋ Cancer	
Excretory Organs	♏ Scorpio	♇ Pluto
Eye (Left of Male)		☽ Moon
Eye (Left of Female)		☉ Sun
Eye (Right of Female)		☽ Moon
Eye (Right of Male)		☉ Sun
Eyes (in general)		☉ Sun
F		
Face	♈ Aries	♂ Mars
Fallopian Tubes	♎ Libra	
Feet	♓ Pisces	♆ Neptune
Fingernails	♑ Capricorn	♄ Saturn
Fingers	♊ Gemini	☿ Mercury
G		
Gall Bladder	♍ Virgo	
Generative Organs		♇ Pluto
Gonad Glands	♏ Scorpio	
H		
Hair	♑ Capricorn	♄ Saturn
Hands	♊ Gemini	☿ Mercury
Head	♈ Aries	♂ Mars
Hearing (Sense of)	♊ Gemini	♄ Saturn
Heart	♌ Leo	☉ Sun
Hips	♐ Sagittarius	♃ Jupiter
I		
Intestines (large)	♏ Scorpio	
Intestines (small)	♍ Virgo	☿ Mercury
J		
Jaw (Lower)	♉ Taurus	
Jaw (Upper)	♈ Aries	
Joints	♑ Capricorn	♄ Saturn
Jugular Vein	♉ Taurus	

Part of Body	Ruling Sign	Ruling Planet
K		
Kidneys	♎ Libra	♀ Venus
Kneecaps	♑ Capricorn	
Knees	♑ Capricorn	♄ Saturn
L		
Larynx	♉ Taurus	☿ Mercury
Legs (lower)	♒ Aquarius	
Legs (upper)	♐ Sagittarius	
Liver	♐ Sagittarius	♃ Jupiter
Lungs	♊ Gemini	☽ Moon
Lymphatic Fluids		☽ Moon
Lymphatic Process	♓ Pisces	
M		
Mouth	♉ Taurus	
Mucous Membranes	♓ Pisces	
Mucus	♓ Pisces	
Muscles		♂ Mars
N		
Nasal Passages		♇ Pluto
Navel		☿ Mercury
Neck	♉ Taurus	
Nerve Fibers	♊ Gemini	
Nervous System (autonomic)		♅ Uranus
Nervous System	♊ Gemini	☿ Mercury
Nose		♂ Mars
O		
Ovaries	♏ Scorpio	♀ Venus
Oxygenation of Blood	♊ Gemini	
P		
Palate		♀ Venus
Pancreas	♍ Virgo	♃ Jupiter
Pelvic Area	♏ Scorpio	
Pelvis		♄ Saturn
Penis		♂ Mars
Pharynx	♉ Taurus	
Phlegm	♓ Pisces	

Part of Body	Ruling Sign	Ruling Planet
Pineal Gland	♓ Pisces	♆ Neptune
Pituitary Gland	♒ Aquarius	♅ Uranus
Prostate Gland	♏ Scorpio	♇ Pluto
R		
Rectum	♏ Scorpio	
Red Blood Cells		♂ Mars
Respiratory System	♊ Gemini	☿ Mercury
Ribs (Lower)	♋ Cancer	
Ribs (Upper)	♊ Gemini	
S		
Saliva		♀ Venus
Salivary Glands	♉ Taurus	
Sciatic Nerve	♐ Sagittarius	
Sensory Perception		☿ Mercury
Sex Organs (Male)	♏ Scorpio	♂ Mars
Sex Organs (Female)	♏ Scorpio	♀ Venus
Shins	♒ Aquarius	
Shoulders	♊ Gemini	☿ Mercury
Sides	♌ Leo	☉ Sun
Sight (Sense of)	♊ Gemini	☿ Mercury
Sinews		♂ Mars
Sinuses	♈ Aries	♇ Pluto
Skeletal Framework	♑ Capricorn	♄ Saturn
Skin	♎ Libra	♀ Venus
Skull	♈ Aries	♄ Saturn
Smell (Sense of)	♊ Gemini	
Solar Plexus	♍ Virgo	☿ Mercury
Spinal Canal		♆ Neptune
Spinal Cord	♌ Leo	
Spinal Fluid	♌ Leo	☽ Moon
Spine	♌ Leo	☉ Sun
Spleen	♑ Capricorn	♄ Saturn
Stomach	♋ Cancer	☽ Moon
Sweat		♂ Mars
Sweat Glands		♂ Mars
T		
Taste (Sense of)	♊ Gemini	♂ Mars
Tears		♆ Neptune
Teeth	♑ Capricorn	♄ Saturn

Part of Body	Ruling Sign	Ruling Planet
Tendons		♄ Saturn
Testes		♂ Mars
Thighs	♐ Sagittarius	♃ Jupiter
Thoracic Cavity	♊ Gemini	
Throat	♉ Taurus	
Thymus Gland	♊ Gemini	
Thyroid Gland	♉ Taurus	☿ Mercury
Toenails	♑ Capricorn	♄ Saturn
Toes	♓ Pisces	♆ Neptune
Tongue	♉ Taurus	☿ Mercury
Tonsils	♉ Taurus	♇ Pluto
Touch (Sense of)	♊ Gemini	♀ Venus
Trachea	♊ Gemini	☿ Mercury
U		
Ureters	♎ Libra	
Urethra	♎ Libra	
Urine	♎ Libra	♀ Venus
Uterus	♋ Cancer	☽ Moon
V		
Vagina		♀ Venus
Veins		♀ Venus
Vena Cava, Inferior	♌ Leo	
Vena Cava, Superior	♌ Leo	
Vocal Cords	♉ Taurus	

PART VII

PLANETARY RULERSHIP
IN HORARY

Subject	Rulers	Co-Rulers
A		
Abdications	♆ Neptune	
Abductions	♇ Pluto	
Abnormal Behavior	♆ Neptune	
Abortion	♇ Pluto	♂ Mars
Abrasions	♂ Mars	
Abscesses	♂ Mars	♇ Pluto
Abundance	♃ Jupiter	
Accidents	♂ Mars	♅ Uranus
Acting	☉ Sun	
Acupuncture	♂ Mars	
Addict	♆ Neptune	
Administrators	♄ Saturn	
Adolescent	☿ Mercury	
Adornment of Physical Body	♀ Venus	
Adventure	♃ Jupiter	
Advertising	☿ Mercury	
Affidavits	☿ Mercury	
Affluence	♃ Jupiter	
Aggression	♂ Mars	
Agreements (written)	☿ Mercury	
Ailments (chronic)	♄ Saturn	
Air Conditioning	☿ Mercury	♅ Uranus
Aircraft	♅ Uranus	
Airlines	♅ Uranus	
Alcoholism	♆ Neptune	
Alias	♆ Neptune	
Alibis	☿ Mercury	
Allergies	☽ Moon	
Ambition	♄ Saturn	
Ambushes	♇ Pluto	♆ Neptune
Ammunition	♂ Mars	
Amputation	♂ Mars	♇ Pluto
Anesthetics	♆ Neptune	
Anger	♂ Mars	
Animal Husbandry	☿ Mercury	
Annihilation	♇ Pluto	
Annulments	♆ Neptune	
Anonymous Letters	♆ Neptune	♇ Pluto
Antiques	♄ Saturn	
Antiseptics	♆ Neptune	

Subject	Rulers	Co-Rulers
Appendicitis	♂ Mars	
Archeology	♇ Pluto	♄ Saturn
Arguments	♂ Mars	
Arson	♂ Mars	
Art	♀ Venus	
Arthritis	♄ Saturn	
Artifacts	♇ Pluto	♄ Saturn
Artificial Arms	☿ Mercury	
Artificial Breast	☽ Moon	
Artificial Eyes	☿ Mercury	
Artificial Feet	♆ Neptune	
Artificial Hands	☿ Mercury	
Artificial Legs	♃ Jupiter	
Artificial Teeth	♄ Saturn	
Artists	♀ Venus	♆ Neptune
Assassination	♇ Pluto	♂ Mars
Assassins	♆ Neptune	
Assaults	♂ Mars	
Astral Entities	♆ Neptune	
Astrology	♅ Uranus	
Asylums	♆ Neptune	
Atomic Energy	♇ Pluto	
Attacks	♂ Mars	
Attraction	♀ Venus	
Audiences	☿ Mercury	
Aura (human)	♅ Uranus	
Authority Figures	♄ Saturn	
Authors	☿ Mercury	
Automobiles	☿ Mercury	♂ Mars
B		
Babies	☽ Moon	
Bacteria	♂ Mars	
Bankruptcy	♄ Saturn	
Banks	♀ Venus	
Battles	♂ Mars	
Beaches	☽ Moon	
Beautification of Body	♀ Venus	
Bedrooms	♀ Venus	
Beliefs	♃ Jupiter	
Bereavement	♄ Saturn	
Betrayal	♇ Pluto	♆ Neptune

Subject	Rulers	Co-Rulers
Biology	☉ Sun	
Blackmail	♆ Neptune	
Bookkeeping	☿ Mercury	
Books	☿ Mercury	
Boundaries	♄ Saturn	
Burial	♄ Saturn	
Buried Treasure	♇ Pluto	
Busses	☿ Mercury	
C		
Cake	♀ Venus	
Cameras	♆ Neptune	
Candy	♀ Venus	
Cathedrals	♃ Jupiter	
Celebrations	♃ Jupiter	
Cemeteries	♄ Saturn	
Ceremonies	♃ Jupiter	
Certificates	☿ Mercury	
Charitable Institutions	♆ Neptune	
Cheating	♆ Neptune	☿ Mercury
Chemicals	♆ Neptune	
Chemistry	♆ Neptune	
Chiropractic	♄ Saturn	
Choking	☿ Mercury	♄ Saturn
Churches	♃ Jupiter	
Clairvoyance	♆ Neptune	♅ Uranus
Communications	☿ Mercury	
Compulsion	♅ Uranus	♇ Pluto
Computer Programming	☿ Mercury	
Computers	☿ Mercury	
Concentration Camps	♆ Neptune	
Conception	♇ Pluto	
Confection	♀ Venus	
Contact Lenses	☿ Mercury	
Contests	♂ Mars	
Contracts	☿ Mercury	
Cookies	♀ Venus	
Cosmetics	♀ Venus	
Courts	♃ Jupiter	
Craftsmanship	☿ Mercury	
Creativity	☉ Sun	
Cremation	♇ Pluto	

Subject	Rulers	Co-Rulers
Crime	♇ Pluto	
D		
Dancing	♆ Neptune	
Death	♄ Saturn	♇ Pluto
Decaying Matter	♇ Pluto	
Deception	♆ Neptune	
Deeds	☿ Mercury	
Delusion	♆ Neptune	
Democratic Party	♄ Saturn	
Dentistry	♂ Mars	
Dentures	♄ Saturn	
Detectives	♇ Pluto	
Dictators	♇ Pluto	
Discipline	♄ Saturn	
Diseases (incurable)	♅ Uranus	
Diseases (nervous)	☿ Mercury	♅ Uranus
Divorce	♅ Uranus	
Documents	☿ Mercury	
Dreams	♆ Neptune	
Drowning	♆ Neptune	
Drugs	♆ Neptune	
Dying	♇ Pluto	
E		
Ego	☉ Sun	
Electricity	♅ Uranus	
Embezzlement	♆ Neptune	
Employers	♄ Saturn	☉ Sun
Etheric Body	♆ Neptune	
Evidence	☿ Mercury	
Exploration	♃ Jupiter	
Explosions	♂ Mars	♅ Uranus
Exposure	♅ Uranus	
Eyeglasses	☿ Mercury	
F		
Faith	♆ Neptune	
Falls from position	♄ Saturn	
False Teeth	♄ Saturn	
Fame	☉ Sun	
Family	☽ Moon	

Subject	Rulers	Co-Rulers
Father	♄ Saturn	☉ Sun
Federal Bureau of Investigation	♇ Pluto	
Film	♆ Neptune	
Finances	♀ Venus	
Fingerprints	☿ Mercury	
Fire	♂ Mars	
Flooding	♆ Neptune	
Food	☿ Mercury	
Forgers	☿ Mercury	
Fraud	♆ Neptune	
Friends	♅ Uranus	
Frustration	♄ Saturn	
Functions	☽ Moon	
Funerals	♄ Saturn	
G		
Gamblers	♃ Jupiter	
Gambling	♃ Jupiter	
Gardens	♀ Venus	
Gas	♆ Neptune	
Generosity	♃ Jupiter	
Gifts	♃ Jupiter	
Gold	☉ Sun	
Gossips	☿ Mercury	
Guns	♂ Mars	
Gunshots	♂ Mars	
H		
Hallucinations	♆ Neptune	
Hearing Aids	♄ Saturn	
Hidden Scandal	♇ Pluto	
History	♄ Saturn	☿ Mercury
Home	☽ Moon	
Hospitals	♆ Neptune	
Hotels	☽ Moon	
Hurricanes	♅ Uranus	
Husband	☉ Sun	
I		
Impotence	♆ Neptune	♄ Saturn
Infidelity	♆ Neptune	♅ Uranus

Subject	Rulers	Co-Rulers
Insects	♇ Pluto	
Inventors	☿ Mercury	
J		
Jewelry	♀ Venus	
Judge	♃ Jupiter	
Judgement (of others)	♄ Saturn	
Judgement (one's own)	♃ Jupiter	
Judiciousness	♃ Jupiter	
Junk	♆ Neptune	
Justice	♄ Saturn	
K		
Kidnapping	♇ Pluto	♆ Neptune
L		
Lead (metal)	♄ Saturn	
Letters	☿ Mercury	
Liberation	♅ Uranus	
Libraries	☿ Mercury	
Licenses	☿ Mercury	
Lies	☿ Mercury	
Lightning	♅ Uranus	
Limits	♄ Saturn	
Liquids	♆ Neptune	
Liquor	♆ Neptune	
Loss of Employment	♄ Saturn	
Lotteries	♃ Jupiter	
Lover	☉ Sun	
Luck	♃ Jupiter	
M		
Machinery	♂ Mars	☿ Mercury
Magazines	☿ Mercury	
Mail	☿ Mercury	
Manuscripts	☿ Mercury	
Marriage	♀ Venus	
Mathematics	♄ Saturn	☿ Mercury
Mechanical Items	♂ Mars	
Men	☉ Sun	♂ Mars
Menstrual Cycle	☽ Moon	
Merchants	☿ Mercury	

Subject	Rulers	Co-Rulers
Messengers	☿ Mercury	
Mistress	♀ Venus	
Money	♀ Venus	
Motels	☽ Moon	
Mother	☽ Moon	
Motives (hidden)	♆ Neptune	
Mourning	♄ Saturn	
Murder	♇ Pluto	
Musicians	♆ Neptune	♀ Venus
N		
Narcotics	♆ Neptune	
Neuroses	♆ Neptune	
Nuclear Energy	♇ Pluto	
Nursing Homes	♆ Neptune	
O		
Obsession	♇ Pluto	♆ Neptune
Occult Abilities	♆ Neptune	
Oil	♆ Neptune	
Oil Lease Investments	♆ Neptune	
Oil Wells	♆ Neptune	
Old People	♄ Saturn	
Optimism	♃ Jupiter	
Organized Crime	♇ Pluto	
Orphans	♆ Neptune	
P		
Painters	♆ Neptune	
Parties	♀ Venus	
Patents	☿ Mercury	
Pathology	♇ Pluto	
Penal Institutions	♆ Neptune	
Perjury	☿ Mercury	♂ Mars
Pessimism	♄ Saturn	
Petroleum	♆ Neptune	♇ Pluto
Philosophy	♃ Jupiter	
Phobias	♆ Neptune	♅ Uranus
Photography	♆ Neptune	
Physics	♅ Uranus	
Pickpockets	☿ Mercury	
Plots	♇ Pluto	

Subject	Rulers	Co-Rulers
Poets	♆ Neptune	
Poisons	♆ Neptune	
Police	♄ Saturn	
Power	♇ Pluto	
Pregnancy	☽ Moon	
Presidents	☉ Sun	
Prisoner of War Camps	♆ Neptune	
Prostitution	♇ Pluto	
Psychiatry	☿ Mercury	♅ Uranus
Psychic Senses	♆ Neptune	
Psychic phenomena	♆ Neptune	♅ Uranus
Psychology	♇ Pluto	
Psychoneurosis	♆ Neptune	
Psychoses	♆ Neptune	
Publishing	♃ Jupiter	
Purses	♀ Venus	
Q		
Quarrels	♂ Mars	
Querent	☽ Moon	
R		
Rape	♇ Pluto	
Real Estate	♄ Saturn	
Reclusiveness	♆ Neptune	
Reformers	♅ Uranus	
Relatives	☿ Mercury	
Religion	♃ Jupiter	
Religious Sects	♆ Neptune	
Republican Party	♃ Jupiter	
Repulsion	♄ Saturn	
Restriction	♄ Saturn	
Retirement Places	♆ Neptune	
Revolutionary	♅ Uranus	
Revolutions	♅ Uranus	
Riots	♇ Pluto	
Rumors	☿ Mercury	
S		
Safe Deposit Boxes	♀ Venus	
Safes	♀ Venus	
Scandal	♇ Pluto	

Subject	Rulers	Co-Rulers
Seclusion	♆ Neptune	
Secrets	♆ Neptune	♇ Pluto
Sedatives	♆ Neptune	
Senility	♄ Saturn	
Separation	♅ Uranus	
Sexual Desire	♂ Mars	
Silver	☽ Moon	
Singing	♀ Venus	
Snakes	♇ Pluto	
Social Centers	♀ Venus	
Space Craft	♅ Uranus	
Sterilization (sexual)	♂ Mars	♄ Saturn
Storms	♅ Uranus	
Strife	♂ Mars	
Suicide	♆ Neptune	
Surgery	♂ Mars	
Sweets	♀ Venus	
Synthetics	♆ Neptune	
T		
Taxes	♇ Pluto	
Teachers	☿ Mercury	♃ Jupiter
Terrorists	♇ Pluto	♂ Mars
Tests	☿ Mercury	
Time	♄ Saturn	
Tornados	♅ Uranus	
Travel	☿ Mercury	♃ Jupiter
Treasonous Acts	♆ Neptune	
Treaties	☿ Mercury	♀ Venus
Tutors	☿ Mercury	♃ Jupiter
U		
Universities	♃ Jupiter	
V		
Vacations	♀ Venus	
Vermin	♇ Pluto	
Violence	♂ Mars	
Virility	☉ Sun	♂ Mars
Viruses	♇ Pluto	

Subject	Rulers	Co-Rulers
Vitality (physical)	☉ Sun	
Vitality (of questioned matter)	☉ Sun	
W		
War	♂ Mars	
Water	♆ Neptune	
Weapons	♂ Mars	
Welfare Programs	♆ Neptune	
Wife	☽ Moon	
Women	☽ Moon	♀ Venus
X		
X-rays	♅ Uranus	♇ Pluto
Y		
Young Females	♀ Venus	
Young Males	♂ Mars	
Young People	☿ Mercury	

PART VIII

EXAMPLE CHARTS

PREAMBLE

The following charts are a few examples which demonstrate the application of some of the principles covered. They include charts demonstrating the direct house system and the derivative house system, charts showing the application of the stepping principle in both a nonblood relationship and a blood relationship, and the application of an ex-relationship in the horary chart.

DIRECT HOUSE SYSTEM

Data: 5/26/1982, 4:29 PM EDT (20:29 GMT), 34N05, 84W20

Question: Will I make the trip to California this summer?

The querent was hoping to make a trip from her home in the East to California.

The horary 1st house represents the querent and the question. Venus is the significator of the querent (♎ rising), and Saturn, Pluto and Jupiter are co-significators (♄, ♇, ♃ occupying 1st house). The Moon co-rules the question. Since the querent travels very little, she considered the planned trip a long-distance one. The trip is represented by the 9th house (objective) and Mercury is the trip significator (♊ on the 9th house cusp).

Venus (querent ruler) makes no aspect to Mercury (trip ruler). This is an indication that the planned trip will not materialize. Furthermore, Mercury is retrograde in the 9th house, the Moon is void of course, and Saturn, Pluto and Jupiter (querent's co-rulers) are retrograde. These are all additional indications that the querent will change her plans and not make the trip.

Outcome:
Conditions kept forcing the querent to postpone her planned trip, and eventually she cancelled her plans. The trip never did materialize.

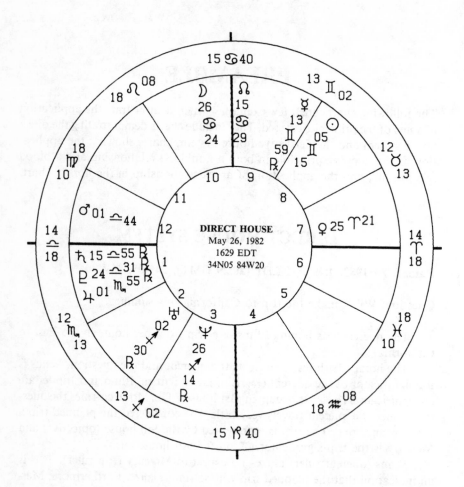

DERIVATIVE HOUSE SYSTEM

Data: 12/7/1982, 8:02 AM EST (13:02 GMT), 34N05, 84W20

Question: Will my uncle survive this heart attack?

The querent received word that her maternal aunt's husband had suffered a massive heart attack.

Jupiter is ruler (♐ rising) and Venus, Mercury, Neptune and Moon are co-rulers of the querent and the question (♀, ☿, ♆ in 1st house). The quesited is the uncle and his house must be located by the derivative house system. The 10th house represents the querent's mother, the 12th house (3rd from mother-10th) represents the mother's sister, and the 6th house (7th from maternal aunt-12th) represents the aunt's spouse (the uncle). The uncle's ruler is Venus (♉ on the cusp).

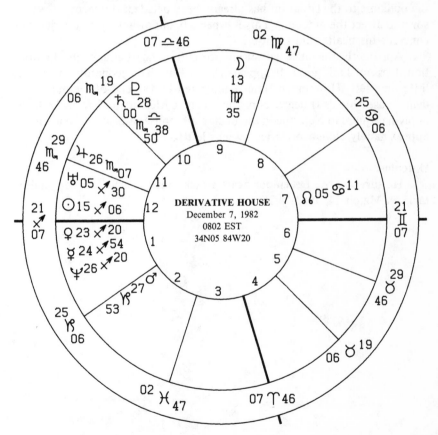

The uncle's house of health (objective) is the 11th house of the horary chart (6th from uncle-6th), ruled by Pluto and co-ruled by Mars (♏ cusp) and Jupiter (♃ in 11th house).

The uncle's house of death is the 1st house of the horary chart (8th from uncle-6th), ruled by Jupiter and co-ruled by Venus, Mercury and Neptune.

Venus, the uncle's significator, is in the 1st house of the horary chart (death and/or surgery-8th from uncle-6th), sextile to Pluto, ruler of his 6th house of health. This is an indication of some recuperative powers and that the uncle's health will improve and he will survive this heart attack. Additionally, the Moon, co-ruler of the question, will trine Mars and sextile Jupiter, co-rulers of the uncle's house of health.

However, the Moon in the 9th house of the horary chart is in the 4th from uncle-6th house, the end of the matter house for the uncle. The Moon will square Mercury, ruler of the end-of-the-matter for the uncle. The Moon will also square Neptune, co-ruler of the uncle's 8th house of death, and Venus, ruler of the uncle. Furthermore, the Moon squares the Sun in the Aunt's house. Uranus, the Aunt's co-ruler, carries a message of fatality by being posited in the nodal degree. The 29th degree on the uncle's Ascendant indicates that the outcome to the situation has already been decided; the seeds have been sown to affect the outcome. This is especially important, since the question concerns his health and his life.

Apparently, the uncle will survive the current heart attack, but the situation does not look good. It appears that his life is in jeopardy and he has little time left. How much time is indicated by the end-of-the-matter cadent/house Moon's 11 degree applying square to Mercury and by the 13 degree applying square to Neptune in the uncle's 8th house of death. The uncle has approximately eleven to thirteen weeks left to live.

Outcome:

He survived the December heart attack, but suffered another fatal attack on March 14, 1983.

STEPPING
NONBLOOD RELATIONSHIP

Data: 2/11/1982, 1:31 PM EST (18:31 GMT), 34N04, 84W18

Question: Shall we go into the flea market booth business? If so, should we choose to set up business at location #1 or location #2? Will the business be successful? Will we make a good profit? If we choose location #1, will the management get air conditioning by the hot summer weather?

Two querents were hoping to open a small business in one of two large flea market locations. Location #1 seemed to be a good location, but was not yet air conditioned, although the management of the flea market promised air conditioning by summer.

The joint querents and the questions are ruled by retrograde Mercury (♊ rising), and the Moon is co-ruler. The quesited business (10th house) is ruled by Neptune (♓ cusp) and co-ruled by Jupiter, which is posited in the Via Combusta. The 12th house of the horary represents the first location (3rd from business-10th, the first objective), and is ruled by Venus, which is in mutual reception with Saturn. The 2nd house of the horary represents the second location (stepping nonblood-3rd from first location-12th, the second objective), and is ruled by the Moon. The significator for the prospective landlord(s) (the horary 7th house) is Jupiter.

Retrograde Mercury (querents) is an indication that the querents will change their minds about this venture. After turning direct, Mercury will square Jupiter (landlords and business). This further indicates adverse challenges involved both in the business and in getting cooperation from the landlords. Neptune (business) receives no aspects from Mercury, indicating that the business will not materialize for the querents.

Mars (horary 11th-business profit, the third objective) will receive a conjunction from the Moon (querents' finances). While Mars is applying to a sextile to Neptune, Mars will go retrograde before the sextile will be completed. The Moon will sextile Neptune (business, which is posited in the 7th house of the horary (landlords). This is an indication that while the business might make a profit, it is more likely that the major portion of that profit would end up with the flea market landlords rather than with the querents. Since the question was asked about one business, the 7th house would represent the landlord at either location.

The first-option location of the flea market business (12th horary house) is signified by Venus (in mutual reception with Saturn) which will receive a square from the Moon. The second-option location (2nd horary house) is signified by the Moon which will conjunct Mars (business profit) and will sextile Neptune (business). The second location presents a better profit potential.

Mercury will sextile Uranus after it goes direct, (both planets connected with machinery and air conditioning), so it is safe to assume a "yes" answer on the air conditioning part of the question, after some delays.

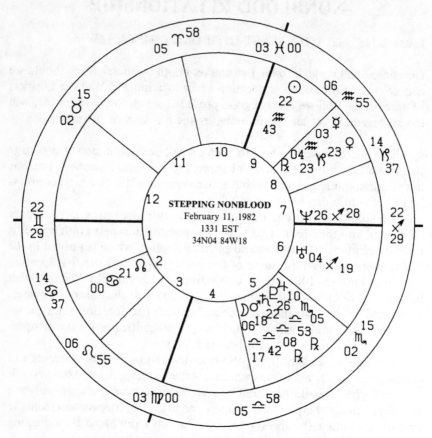

Venus, which will square the Moon, is in mutual reception with Saturn, significator of the landlords' 2nd house of finances (8th of horary). By virtue of the mutual reception, this creates a square to Saturn from the Moon, indicating financial difficulties for the landlords.

The landlord's ongoing sound financial condition is important to the success of all the booths in a flea market. Neptune's position in the landlords' house (horary 7th) points to possible deception on the part of either landlord. Additionally, Mercury squaring Jupiter after it goes direct is an indication of nonagreement between the querents and the landlord.

Outcome:

A disagreement surfaced during negotiations when the landlord for each location refused to agree to allow the querents to carry certain products which would enhance their profits. This was a decisive factor in the querents' decision not to go ahead with either booth.

Subsequent events proved that both landlords had misled the querents regarding the amount of advertisement they planned and the volume of customers expected through the flea market. Other booth renters in both locations were denied refunds of up-front money when they were forced to close down due to lack of business. Neither location prospered.

STEPPING
BLOOD RELATIONSHIP

Data: 5/12/1982, 8:30 PM EDT (00:30 GMT 5/13/1982), 33N57, 84W34

Question: Will my older child be accepted by the school if my younger child is?

The querent wanted to enroll both her young children in a parochial elementary school. There was a possibility that the school might accept the younger child, but not the older one.

The horary 5th house represents the first child (first quesited) and the horary 7th house (blood relation sibling-3rd from child-5th) represents the second child (second quesited). Mars is the significator (♈ cusp) and Venus is the co-significator of the older child (♀ in the 5th). Venus is the significator (♉ cusp) and Mercury is the co-significator of the younger child (☿ in the 7th). Mars and Venus are in mutual reception. Since neither child had been accepted at the time of the question, the horary 3rd house represents the school (the objective). The school's co-significators are Saturn (Capricorn cusp) and Uranus (Aquarius intercepted in 3rd).

Venus (younger child) is posited in the 5th house (older child), and the brothers' significators are in mutual reception. Both conditions are good indicators that the brothers will remain together. Mercury, strong in the dual sign of Gemini and co-ruler of the younger child, is trine to Saturn (school). In addition, Mars (older child) is sextile to Uranus (school). The children will probably both be accepted.

Saturn and Uranus represent the school and are retrograde. Venus, posited in the older child's house and ruler of the younger child, is opposed to Saturn. The Moon is square to Saturn and both are in the nodal degree. All these conditions indicate that this parochial environment may not be the best educational vehicle for the children.

Outcome:

The younger child was accepted and because the school had a policy of accepting all the children in a family, the older child was also accepted. The quality of any school as an educational vehicle cannot be determined for many years.

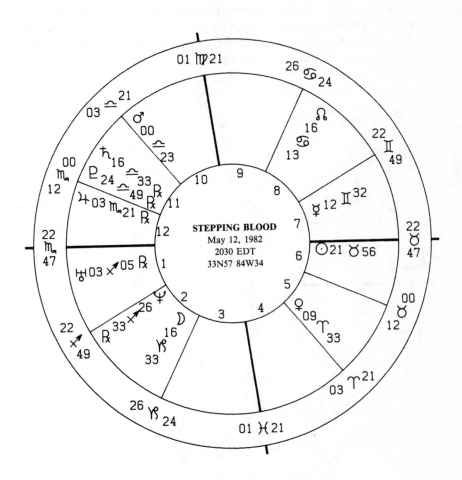

STEPPING BLOOD
May 12, 1982
2030 EDT
33N57 84W34

EX-SPOUSE RELATIONSHIP

Data: 6/23/1982, 9:15 PM EDT (1:15 GMT 6/24/1982), 33N45, 84W23

Question: Will my ex-husband appear in court on July 16, 1982, and pay me the money he owes me?

The querent's ex-husband was several months behind in his child support payments. The querent was seeking court action.

The querent's only relationship to the ex-husband is through their child. Therefore the ex-husband (the quesited) is located in the horary chart through the derivative house system as father of the querent's child (4th from child-5th) or the 8th house of the horary chart.

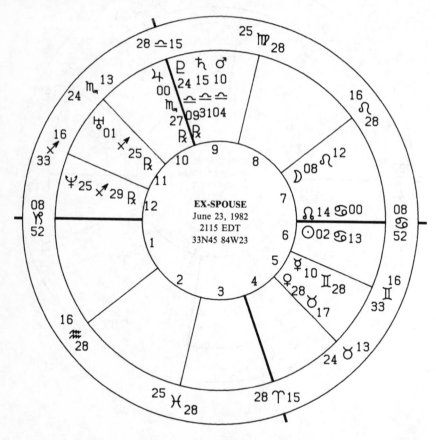

The significator of the querent and the question is Saturn (♑ cusp). The Moon is co-ruler. The ex-husband is signified by the Sun (♌ cusp). The horary 9th represents the ex-husband's financial condition and the courts (the objective), and is signified by Mercury (♍ cusp) and co-signified by Mars, Saturn and Pluto (♂, ♄, ♇ in 9th house). The horary 7th represents the querent's lawyer and is signified by the Moon.

The Sun is square to Mars (husband's money) and Mars will conjunct Saturn, thereby translating the light of the square to Saturn. The Sun square Mars and Saturn shows both the ex-husband's distressed financial condition and the disagreement and conflict between the querent and the ex-husband. It appears that the ex-husband will not show in court nor will he pay the money.

Mercury (ex-husband's money), however, is trine to Saturn (querent), indicating that she will eventually get the money. The Sun (the ex-husband) is in mutual reception with the Moon (querent's lawyer) and the Moon sextiles Mars and Saturn, both posited in the horary 9th house of courts and lawsuits. The efforts of a lawyer will eventually be instrumental in bringing about a settlement between the querent and the ex-husband.

Outcome:

The ex-husband did not appear in court on the set date. Nor did he voluntarily pay the child support payments due. The querent, at this writing, is in the process of seeking remedy through the courts.

AFTERWORD

Our primary goal in writing this book was to compile a dictionary of horary house rulerships. However, in doing so, we were led into areas that we could not have initially foreseen. The entire experience was both humbling and exhilarating.

As previously stated, we have checked many reference sources and have tried to incorporate a consensus of astrological opinion into this book. We hope that our efforts will help to clarify some of the previously unresolved questions and controversies surrounding the judgment of the horary chart.

In the course of our investigation, we realized that there is reason to the derivative house system; that the entire success of the judgment of the horary chart depends upon the proper evaluation of the closest relationship between the querent and the quesited/objective. We learned that there are two methods of stepping to be used, when the question involves like multiple subjects as objectives, depending upon whether the objectives are blood-related or are not blood-related.

We have gained many additional insights into other aspects of horary astrology, which we hope to share in the future. In the meantime, while the stepping methods are unique to the practice of horary astrology, the derivative house system is applicable in all branches of astrology. We hope that the practicing astrologer will find this book useful in determining house rulerships.

Knowledge continues to evolve and horary astrology, along with all other branches of astrology, is subject to ongoing research and development. We hope that astrologers will not just accept the thoughts we have to offer, but will test these theories. We would appreciate hearing from you, our readers, and receiving charts which support or contradict our findings.

Anne and Lillian

BIBLIOGRAPHY

Bills, Rex E. *The Rulership Book*. Richmond, Va.: Macoy Publishing & Masonic Supply Company, Inc., 1971.

Cornell, Howard Leslie. *Encyclopaedia of Medical Astrology*. St. Paul and New York: Llewellyn Publications and Samuel Weiser, Inc., 1972.

David, Geraldine. *A Modern Scientific Textbook on Horary Astrology*. Los Angeles, Ca.: First Temple of Astrology, 1942.

Dean, Geoffrey. *Recent Advances in Natal Astrology*. Southampton, England: The Camelot Press, 1977.

De Long, Sylvia. *The Art of Horary Astrology in Practice*. Tempe, Az.: American Federation of Astrologers, Inc.

De Luce, Robert. *Horary Astrology*. New York: ASI Publishers, Inc., 1932.

de Vore, Nicholas. *Encyclopedia of Astrology*. Totowa, New Jersey: Littlefield, Adams & Co., 1976.

Doane, Doris Chase. *Astrology Rulerships*. Redondo Beach, Ca.: Foundation of Scientific Spiritual Understanding, 1970.

George, Llewellyn. *A to Z Horoscope Maker and Delineator*. St. Paul, Mn.: Llewellyn Publications, 1974.

Goldstein-Jacobson, Ivy M. *Simplified Horary Astrology*. Alhambra, Ca.: Frank Severy Publishing, 1960.

Green, Liz. *Relating*. New York: Samuel Weiser, Inc.

Heindel, Max and Heindel, Augusta Foss. *The Message of the Stars*. London, England: L.N. Fowler & Co., Ltd., 1973.

Hone, Margaret E.. *The Modern Textbook of Astrology*. London, Eng.: L. N. Fowler & Co., Ltd., 1951.

Jansky, Robert Carl. *Astrology, Nutrition & Health*. Rockport, Mass.: Para Research, Inc., 1977.

Moore, Marcia and Douglas, Mark. *Astrology, The Divine Science*. York Harbor, Maine: Arcane Publications.

Ptolemy. *Ptolemy's Tetrabiblos*. Trans. by J. M. Ashmand. North Hollywood, Ca.: Symbols & Signs, 1976.

Raphael. *Raphael's Horary Astrology*. London, Eng.: W. Foulsham & Co., 1897.

Simmonite, Dr. W. J. *Horary Astrology*. Tempe, Az.: American Federation of Astrologers, Inc., 1950.

Sepharial. *The Manual of Astrology*. New York, N.Y.: Wholesale Book Corp., 1972.

Watters, Barbara H.. *Horary Astrology and the Judgement of Events*. Washington, DC: Valhalla Paperbacks, Ltd., 1973.

INDEX

NOTES

NOTES

THE HORARY REPORT

To complement our publication of *The Horary Reference Book*, Astro is offering a new option for customers. This report will make the analysis of horary charts much simpler!

The Horary Report includes a horoscope for the moment of the question. (If you wish **only** the $2.00 wheeled horoscope, order your horary charts as you would any natal chart.) Our Horary Report will **also** provide listings of the following information:

1. All of the **Moon's aspects** until it changes sign. **Plus,** a listing of the aspects ten degrees into the next sign if the Moon was late in a sign.

2. All traditional horary aspects (♂ ✶ □ △ ☍) **Plus,** aspects of quincunx, parallel and contra-parallel (used by many horary astrologers) are listed as well.

3. Any situations involving the **translation of light, collection of light,** or **refranation** are included.

4. **Retrograde planets** will be noted for your use.

5. Conditions which indicate **strictures against judgment** will be brought to your attention.

6. Planets in **mutual reception, Via Combusta or the nodal degree** will be clearly indicated on the report.

This report summarizes all the important information for judging your horary chart on one 8½ by 11 piece of paper. Astro intends to make ascertaining the answers to your questions as effortless as possible!

All that is required of customers is to mail in the correct data (day, month, year, time and place) of each horary question to Astro. The charge for each **Horary Report** is $3.00 (plus $2.00 handling per order from Astro).

Whether you are an old hand at horary and just want to save a little time in calculations — or you are a beginner looking for an easy-to-follow approach to horary, this option is for you!

Write those questions down and send for your **Horary Report** today!

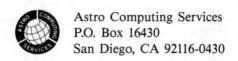

Astro Computing Services
P.O. Box 16430
San Diego, CA 92116-0430

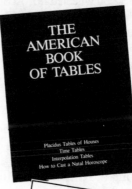
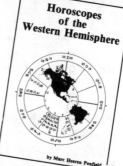

We calculate... You delineate!

CHART CALCULATIONS

Natal Chart wheel with planet/sign glyphs 2.00
Arabic Parts All traditional parts and more 1.00
Asteroids ⚳ ⚴ ⚵ ⚶ in wheel + aspects/midpoints .50
Asteroids ⚳ ⚴ ⚵ ⚶ + 15 new ones for 20th century only 1.00
Astrodynes Power, harmony and discord 2.00
Concentric Wheels Any 3 charts available in wheel format may be combined into a '3 wheeler' 3.00
Deduct $1.00 for each chart ordered as a separate wheel.
Fixed Stars Robson's 110 fixed stars with aspects 1.00
Fortune Finder 97 ancient, 99 modern Arabic Parts 2.00
Graphic Midpoint Sort highlights groupings. **Specify integer divisions of 360°** (1 = 360°, 4 = 90°, etc.) 1.00
Harmonic Chart John Addey type. **Specify harmonic number** 2.00
Harmonic Positions 30 consecutive sets. **Specify starting harmonic #** 1.00
Heliocentric Charts Sun-centered positions 2.00
Horary Report Based on the Horary Reference Book 3.00
House Systems Comparison for 9 systems .50
Local Space Planet compass directions (azimuth & altitude) .50
Locality Map USA, World, Europe, S. Amer., Far East, Austl., Middle East and Africa map — choice of rise, set, and culmination lines or Asc., Desc., MC, IC lines for each map 6.00
Midpoint Structures Midpoint aspects + midpoints in 45° and 90° sequence 1.00
Rectification Assist 10 same-day charts. **Specify starting time, time increment, e.g., 6 AM, every 20 minutes** 10.00
Relocation Chart Specify original birth data & new location 2.00
Uranian Planets + halfsums .50
Uranian Sensitive Points (includes Uranian Planets) 3.50

INTERPRETATION REPORTS

Planetary Profile (Complete) 20-30 pages 18.00
Both include natal chart. (Concise) about 15 pages 12.00
A major breakthrough in an integrated natal interpretation report.
Astrological Annotation gives astrological factors used (if requested) N/C
Each of the following sections of the Planetary Profile may be ordered separately: basic identity, overview, work & career, mind, relationships, values & beliefs, sex, money, children, parents, growth, future themes. each 2.00
Sexual Expression & Enrichment Report 6.00
Interpretive Romance Report Specify Natal Data for 2 births. Romance Oriented. See Themes for Two for other relationships. 8.00
Themes For Two report includes composite chart. Specify Natal Data for two births and location. Suitable for any relationship. 8.00
Interpretive Transits. Specify Starting Month
Outer Planets ♃♄♅♆♇ Hard Aspects Only ☌☍□∠⚼ 12 mos. 8.00
Outer Planets ♃♄♅♆♇ Soft & Hard Aspects △⚹⚻☌☍□∠⚼ 12 mos. 10.00
9 Planets Hard Aspects Only 6 mos. 15.00/12 mos. 25.00
9 Planets Soft & Hard Aspects 6 mos. 18.00/12 mos. 30.00

HUMAN RELATIONSHIPS

Chart Comparison (Synastry) All aspects between the two sets of planets plus house positions of one in the other 1.50
Composite Chart Rob Hand-type. **Specify location** 2.00
Relationship Chart Erected for space-time midpoint 2.00

COLOR CHARTS

4-Color Wheel Any chart we offer in new, aesthetic format with color coded aspect lines 2.00
Local Space Map 4-color on 360° circle 2.00
Custom 6" Disk for any harmonic (laminated, you cut out) overlays on our color wheel charts 4.00
Plotted Natal Dial Use with custom 6" Disk. **Specify harmonic #** 2.00

COLOR CHARTS (continued)

Custom Graphic Ephemeris in 4 colors. **Specify harmonic, zodiac, starting date.** varied prices
Dynamic Astrology Graph 1 year 3.00

FUTURE TRENDS

Progressed Chart secondary, quotidian, tertiary or minor. **Specify progressed day, month and year** 2.00
Secondary Progressions Day-by-day progressed aspects to natal and progressed planets, ingresses and parallels by month, day and year. **Specify starting year, MC by solar arc (standard) or RA of mean Sun** 5 years 3.00
10 years 5.00
85 years 15.00
Minor or Tertiary Progressions Minor based on lunar-month-for-a-year, tertiary on day-for-a-lunar-month. **Specify year, MC by solar arc (standard) or RA of mean sun** 1 year 2.00
Progressed Lifetime Lunar Phases a la Dane Rudhyar 5.00
Solar Arc Directions Day-by-day solar arc directed aspects to the natal planets, house and sign ingresses by month, day and year. **Specify starting year.** Asc. and Vertex arc directions available at same prices 1st 5 years 1.00
Each add'l 5 years .50
Primary Arc Directions (Includes speculum) 5 years 1.50
Specify starting year Each add'l 5 years .50
Transits by all planets except Moon. Date and time of transiting aspects/ingresses to natal chart. **Specify starting month.** Moon-only transits available at same prices. 6 mos. 7.00
OR 12 mos. 12.00
Summary only 6 mos. 3.50
Summary only 12 mos. 6.00
Calendar Format (9 planets OR Moon only) 6 mos. 7.00
Calendar Format (9 planets OR Moon only) 12 mos. 12.00
Calendar Format (Moon & planets) 6 mos. 12.00
Calendar Format (Moon & planets) 12 mos. 20.00
Returns in wheel format. All returns can be precession corrected. **Specify place, Sun-return year, Moon-return month, planet-return month/year.** Solar, Lunar or Planet 2.00
13 Lunar 15.00

ALL ABOUT ASTROLOGY

Booklets to explain options. (Cal. residents add 6% sales tax)
The Art of Chart Comparison 2.00
What Are Astrolocality Maps? 2.00
The Eastpoint and the Anti-Vertex 2.00
Interpreting Composite And Relationship Charts 1.50
What Are Winning Transits? 1.50
The Zodiac: A Historical Survey 2.00

POTPOURRI

Astromusical Cassettes See our catalog varied prices
Winning!! Timing for gamblers, exact planet and transiting house cusps based on Joyce Wehrman's system. Specify location, dates of speculation, natal data. 1-7 days (per day) 3.00
8 or more days (per day) 2.00
Winning Overview Planetary transits with + and − for planning speculation 6 mos. 12.00/12 mos. 20.00
Biorhythms Chart the 23-day, 28-day and 33-day cycles in black/white graph format. Printed { per mo. .50 / 12 mos. 4.00 }
4-Color Graph on our plotter Color 6 mos. 2.00
Custom House Cusps Table Specify latitude ° ′ ″ or city 10.00
Custom American Ephemeris Page Any month, 2500 BC-AD 2500. **Specify zodiac (Sidereal includes RA & dec.)**
One mo. geocentric or two mos. heliocentric 5.00
One year ephemeris (**specify beginning mo. yr.**) 50.00
One year heliocentric ephemeris 25.00
Fertility Report The Jonas method for 1 year 3.00
Specify starting month.
Lamination of 1 or 2 sheets (Back to back) 1.00
Transparency (B/W) of any chart or map. Ordered at same time 1.00
Handling charge per order 2.00

SAME DAY SERVICE — Ask for Free Catalog
ASTRO COMPUTING SERVICES, Inc.
P.O. BOX 16430
SAN DIEGO, CA 92116-0430
NEIL F. MICHELSEN

(Prices Subject to Change)